# WHITE NIGHT

## AN ADMAN'S STORY

## WRITTEN + ILLUSTRATED BY
## KEVIN SACCO

### PUBLISHED BY
### SLG PUBLISHING
## 44 RACE STREET SAN JOSE, CA 95126
#### WWW.SLGPUBS.COM

HAROLD'S SHOWSPOT

THIS STORY IS A FICTION INSPIRED BY MY LATE FATHER.
HE WORKED AS A COPYWRITER DURING THE "GOLDEN AGE" OF
ADVERTISING. HE CREATED SOME MEMORABLE AD CAMPAIGNS ONE
OF WHICH WAS FOR AJAX LAUNDRY DETERGENT FEATURING A WHITE
KNIGHT.

HE BELIEVED IN THE "EUREKA" MOMENT THAT WOULD COME AFTER
COPIOUS RESEARCH AND DISCIPLINED BRAINSTORMING.

HE WAS A WONDERFUL STORYTELLER. I LISTENED RAPTLY.
THIS STORY IS MY GUESS ABOUT ONE OF HIS "EUREKA MOMENTS".

I'VE CHANGED HIS NAME IN THIS STORY TO ZEPPO
ABANDANDO, THE PROTAGANIST OF HIS NEVER
PUBLISHED NOVEL "TWO CENTS CHEAPER".

KEVIN SACCO.

FOR RONNIE WHO
KNEW THE FELLOW.

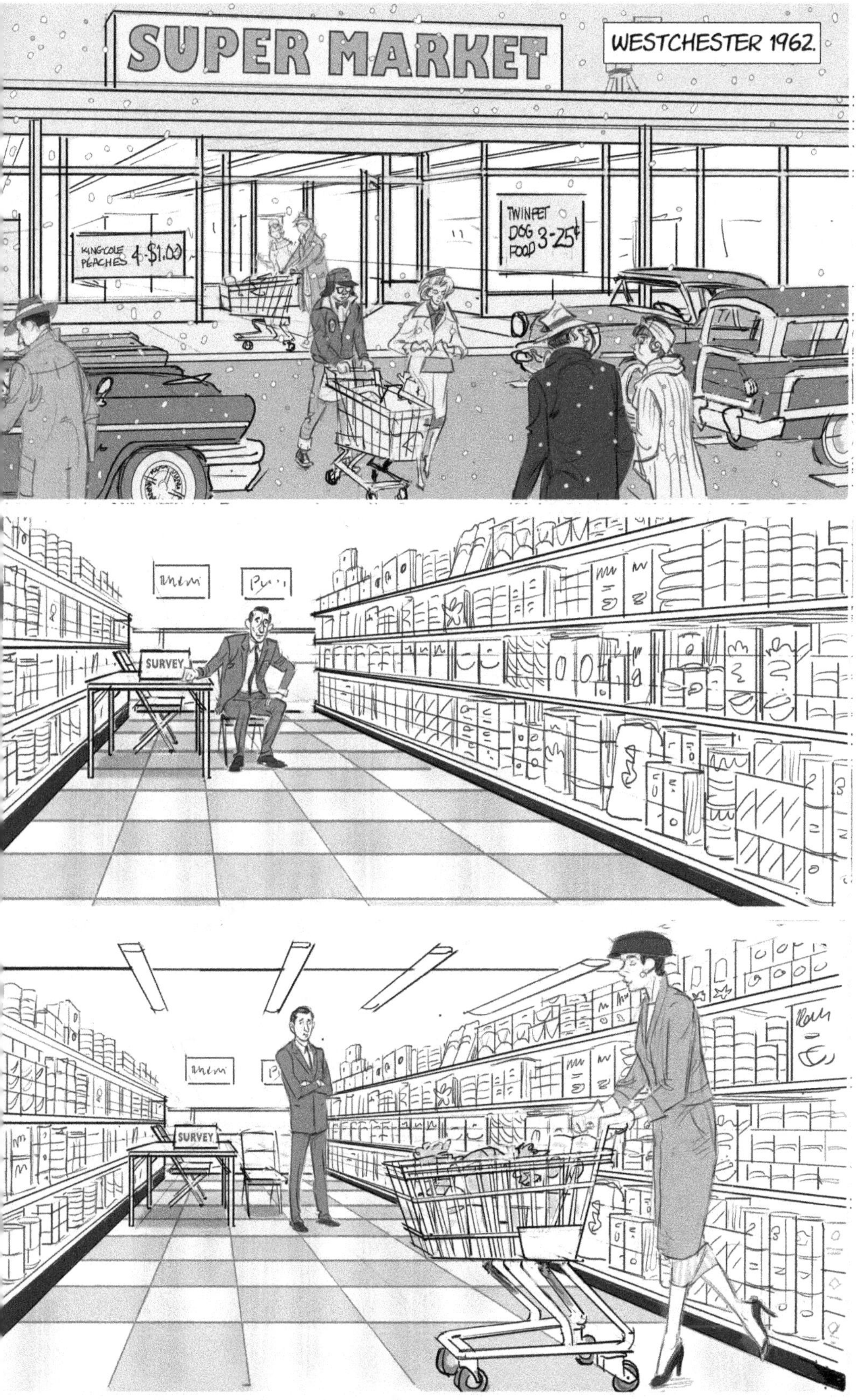
SUPER MARKET
WESTCHESTER 1962.
KING COLE PEACHES 4-$1.00
TWINPET DOG FOOD 3-25¢
SURVEY
SURVEY

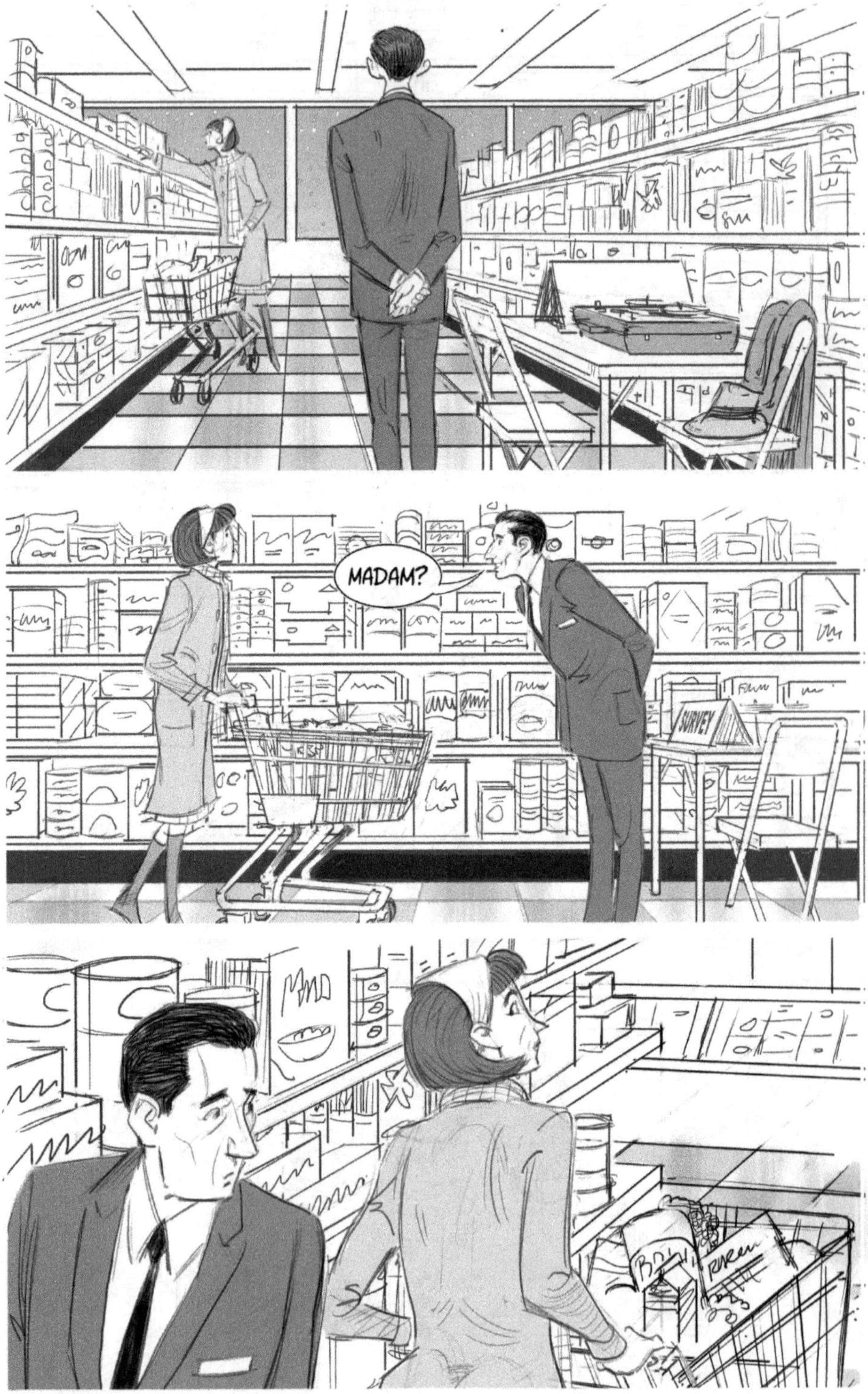
MADAM?
SURVEY

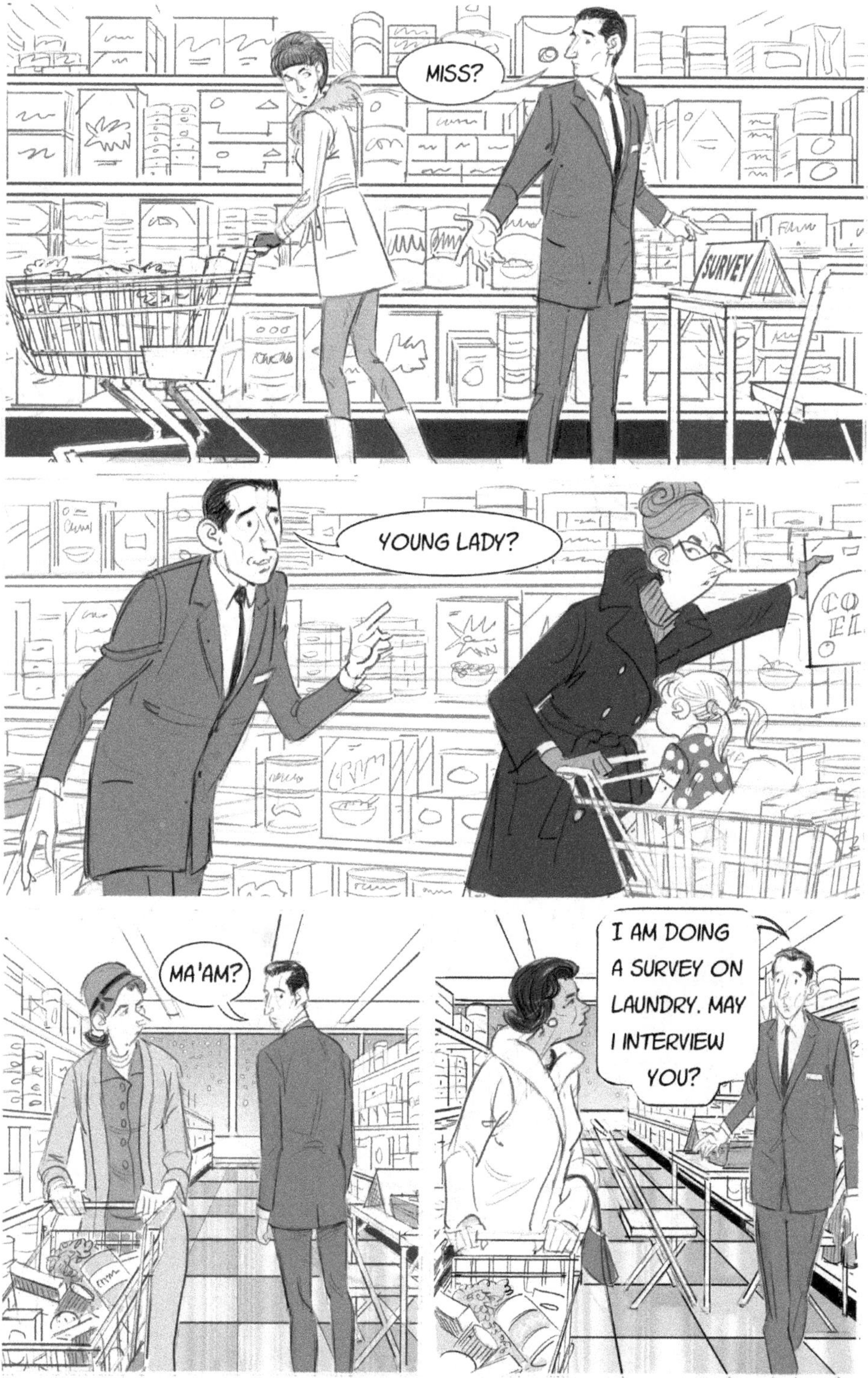
MISS?
SURVEY
YOUNG LADY?
MA'AM?
I AM DOING A SURVEY ON LAUNDRY. MAY I INTERVIEW YOU?

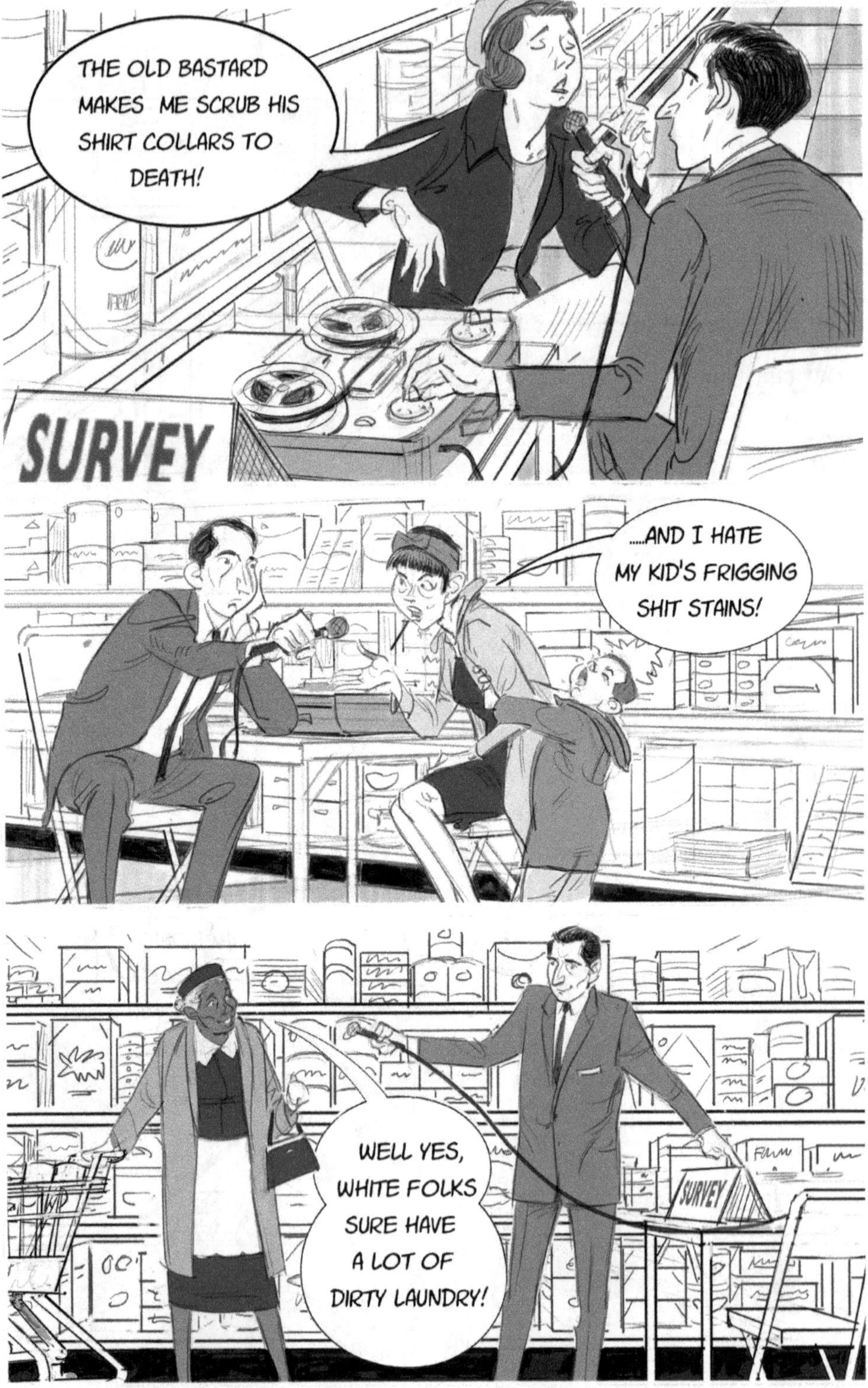
THE OLD BASTARD MAKES ME SCRUB HIS SHIRT COLLARS TO DEATH!
SURVEY
....AND I HATE MY KID'S FRIGGING SHIT STAINS!
SURVEY
WELL YES, WHITE FOLKS SURE HAVE A LOT OF DIRTY LAUNDRY!

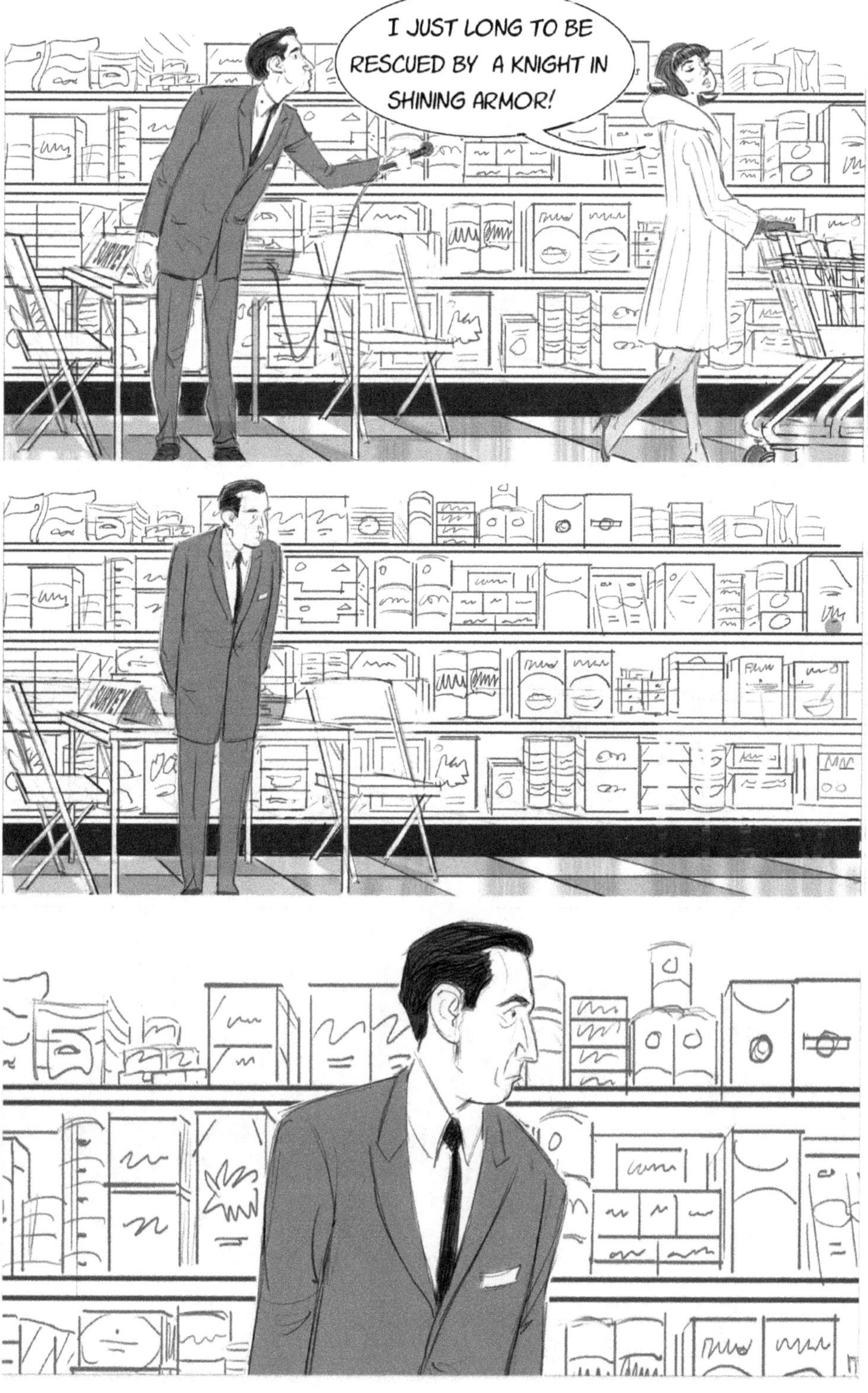
I JUST LONG TO BE RESCUED BY A KNIGHT IN SHINING ARMOR!

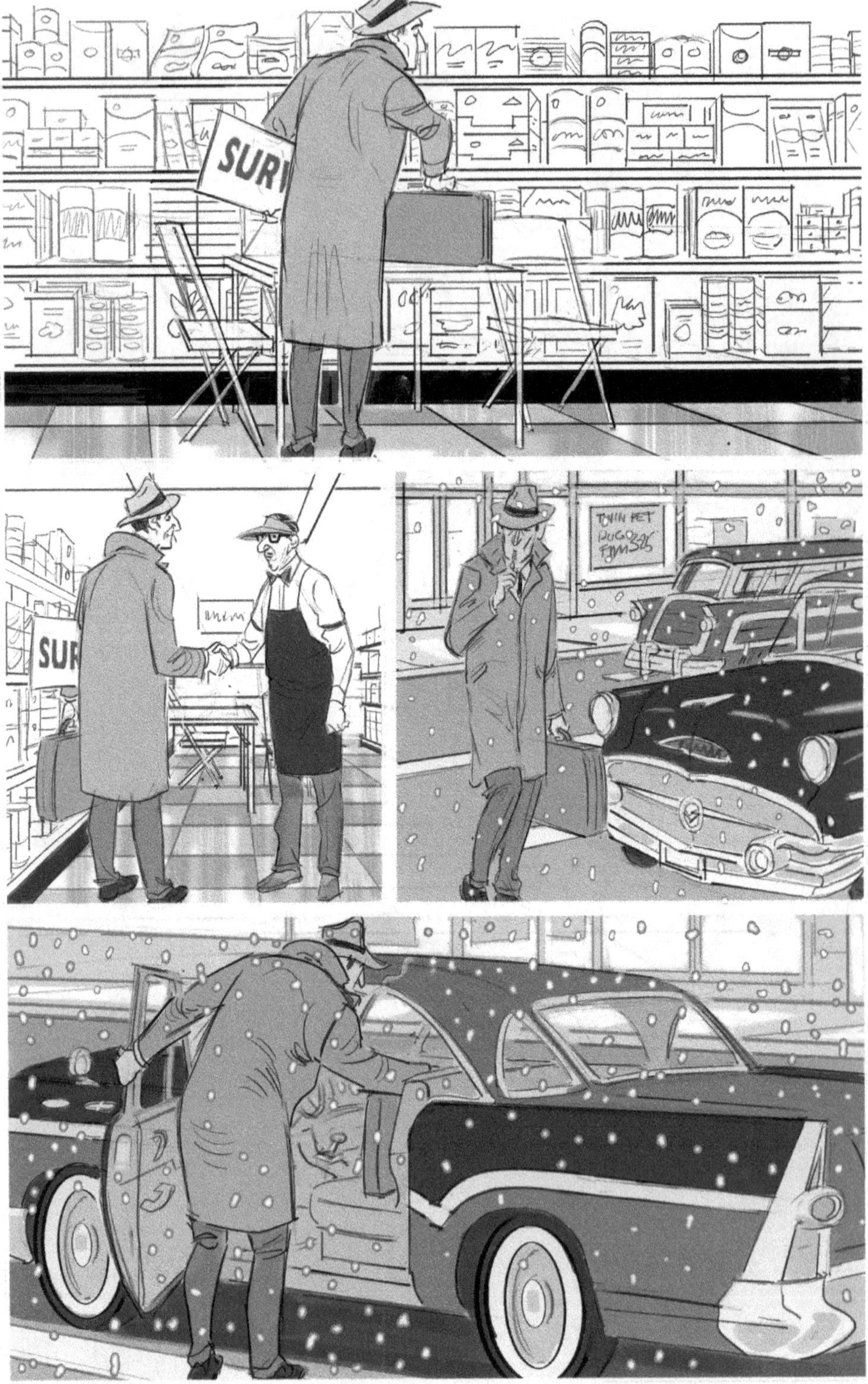

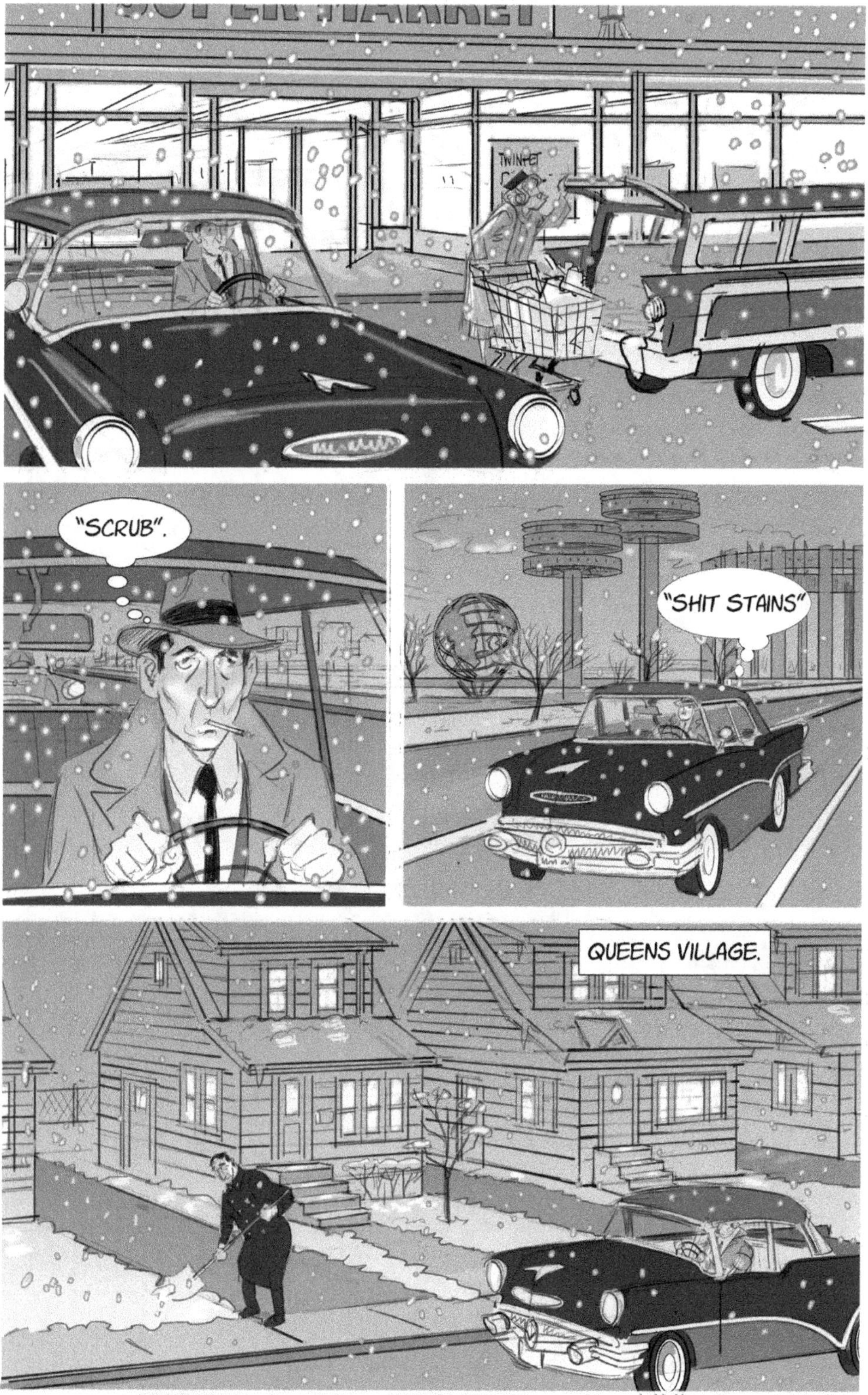
"SCRUB".
"SHIT STAINS"
QUEENS VILLAGE.

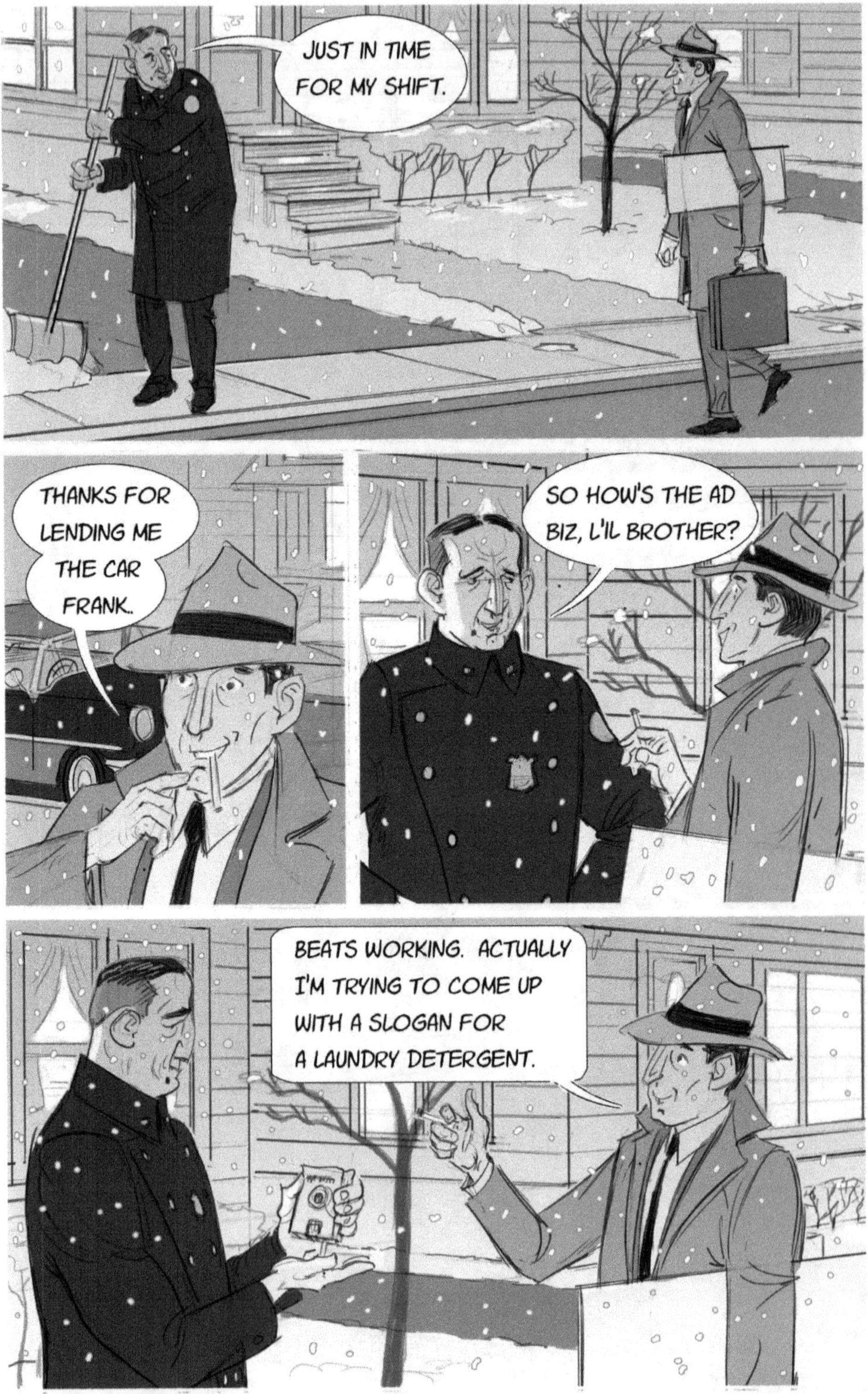
JUST IN TIME FOR MY SHIFT.
THANKS FOR LENDING ME THE CAR FRANK..
SO HOW'S THE AD BIZ, L'IL BROTHER?
BEATS WORKING. ACTUALLY I'M TRYING TO COME UP WITH A SLOGAN FOR A LAUNDRY DETERGENT.

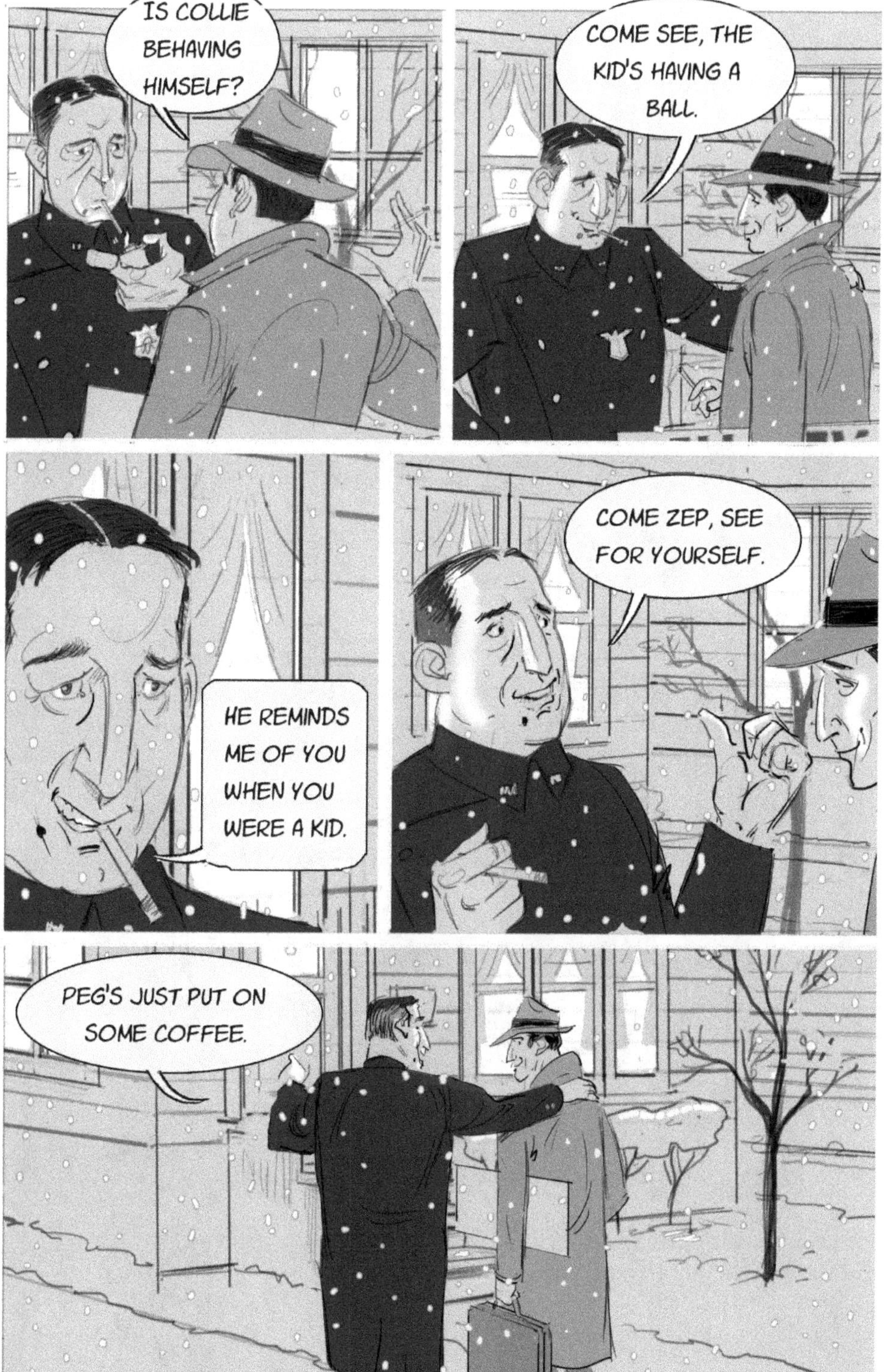
IS COLLIE BEHAVING HIMSELF?
COME SEE, THE KID'S HAVING A BALL.
HE REMINDS ME OF YOU WHEN YOU WERE A KID.
COME ZEP, SEE FOR YOURSELF.
PEG'S JUST PUT ON SOME COFFEE.

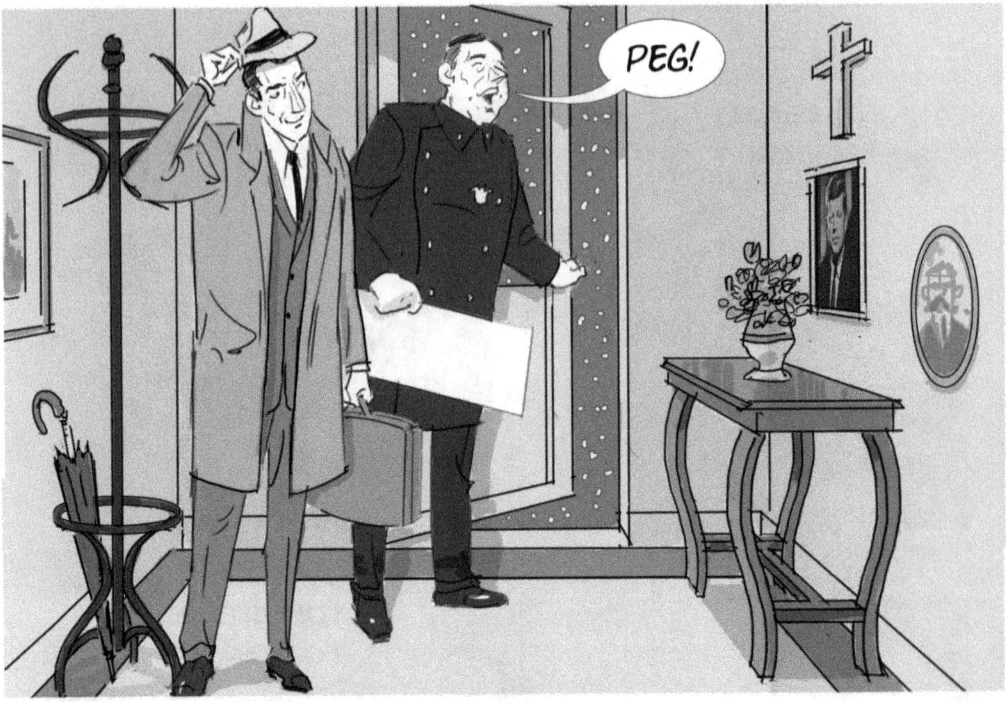
PEG!
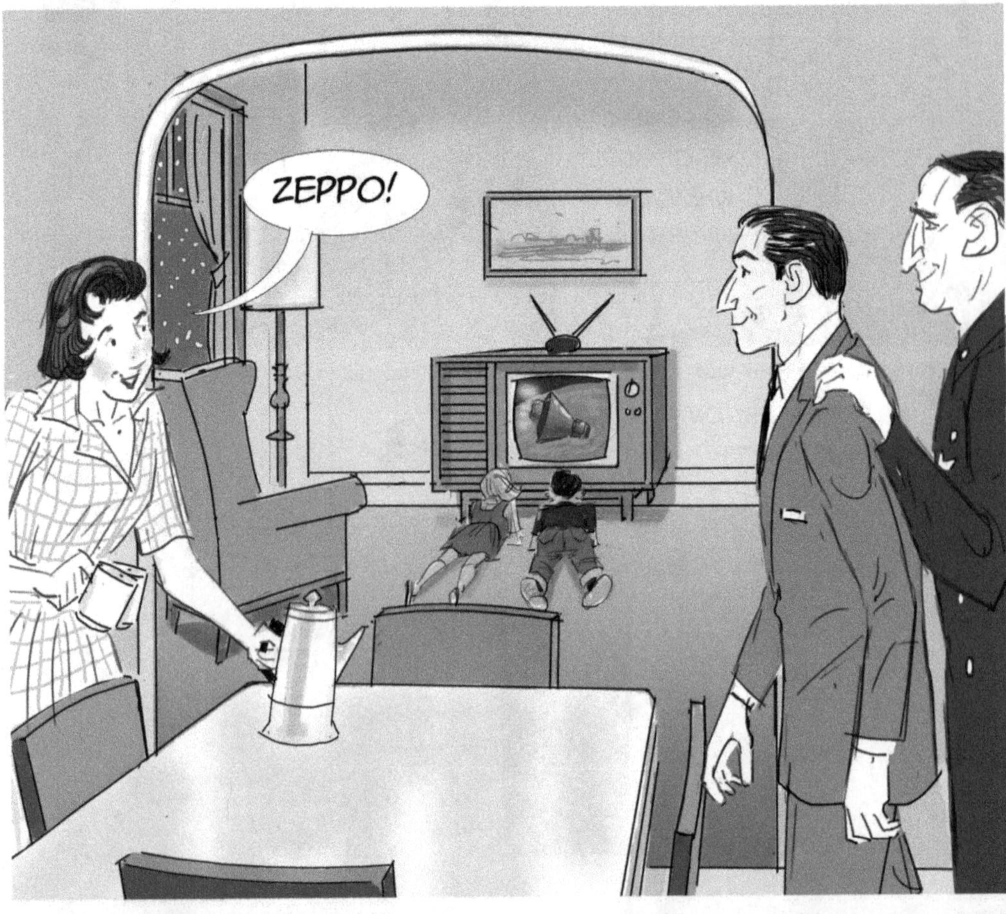
ZEPPO!

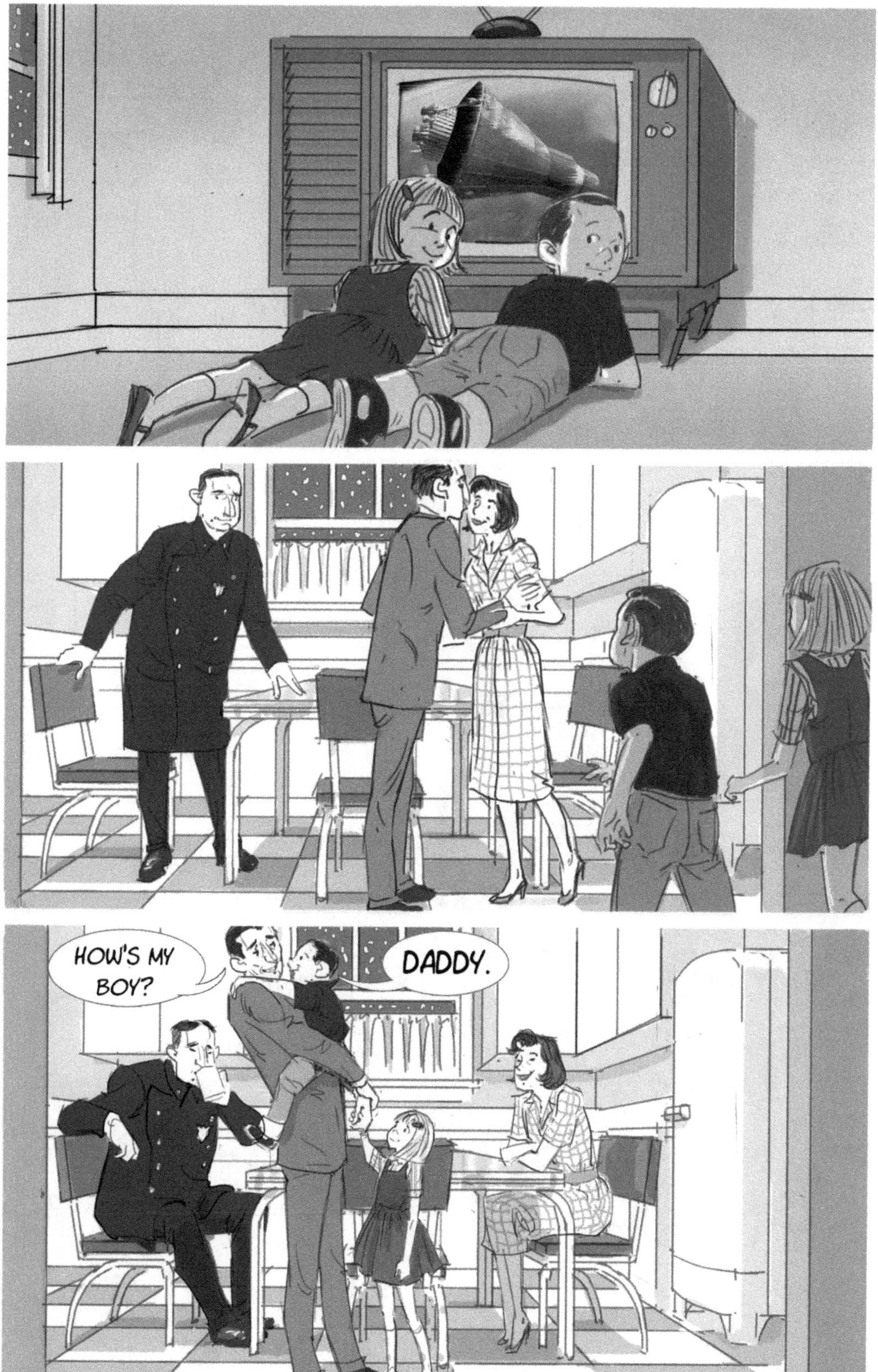
HOW'S MY BOY?
DADDY.

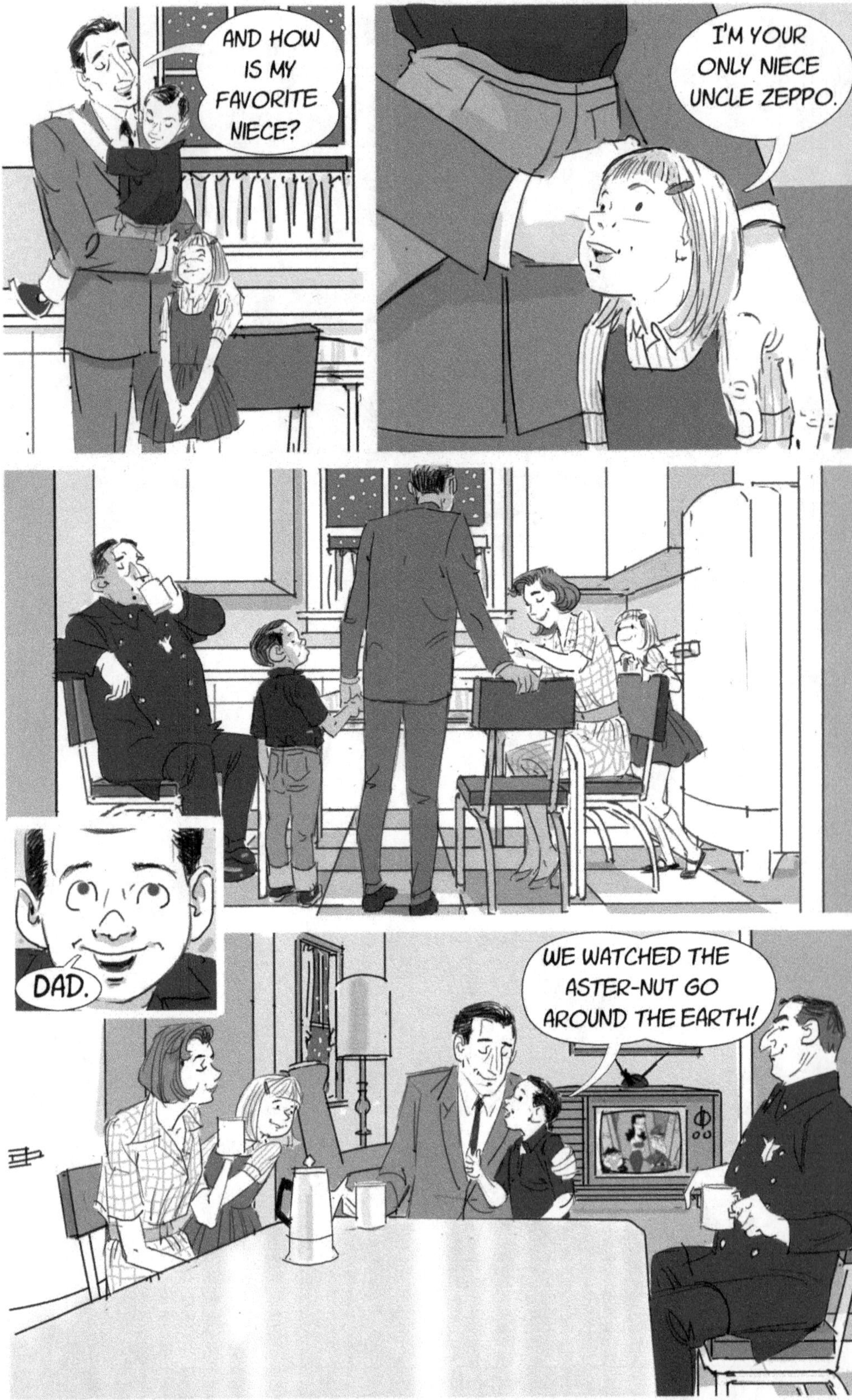
AND HOW IS MY FAVORITE NIECE?
I'M YOUR ONLY NIECE UNCLE ZEPPO.
DAD.
WE WATCHED THE ASTER-NUT GO AROUND THE EARTH!

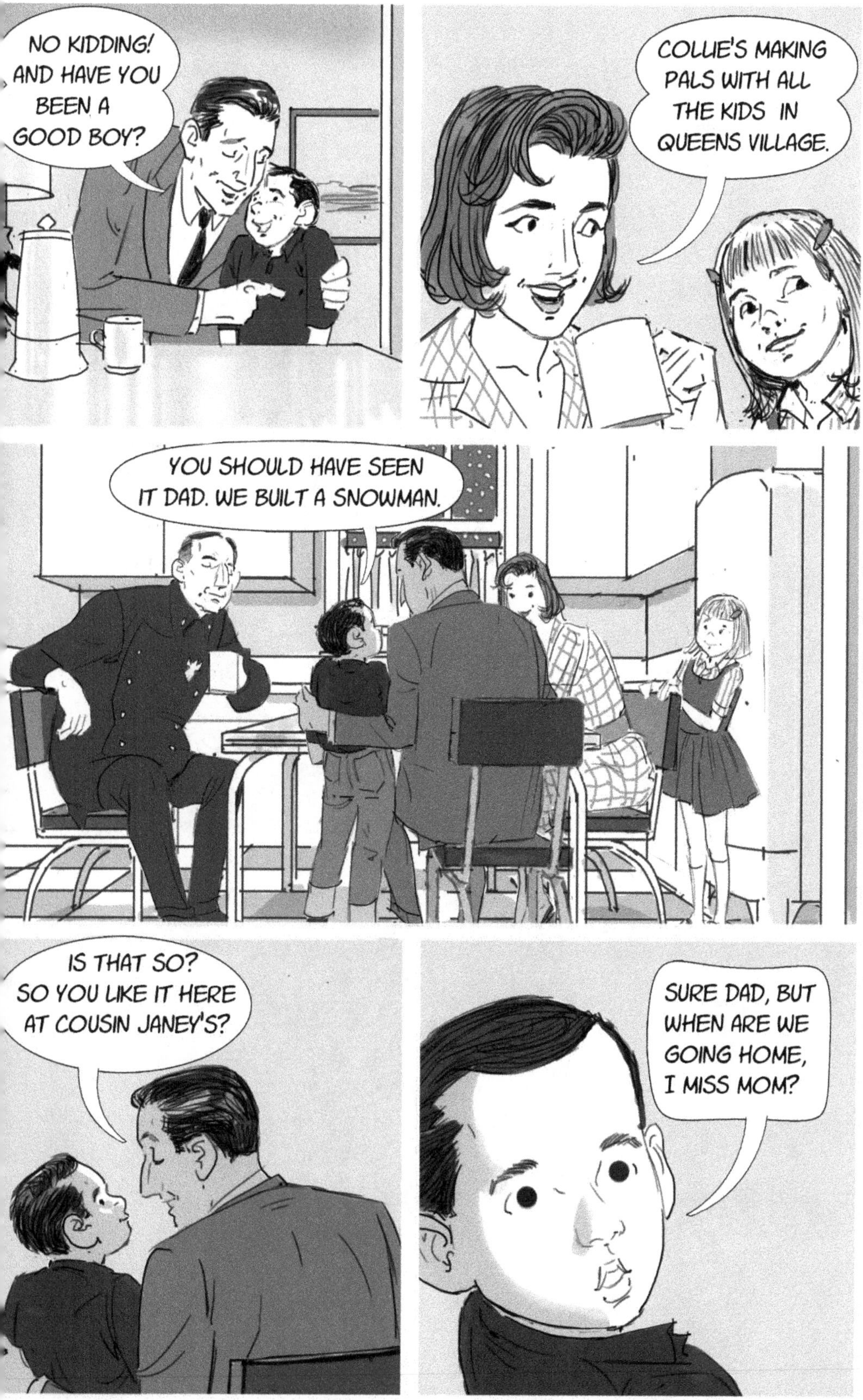
NO KIDDING! AND HAVE YOU BEEN A GOOD BOY?
COLLIE'S MAKING PALS WITH ALL THE KIDS IN QUEENS VILLAGE.
YOU SHOULD HAVE SEEN IT DAD. WE BUILT A SNOWMAN.
IS THAT SO? SO YOU LIKE IT HERE AT COUSIN JANEY'S?
SURE DAD, BUT WHEN ARE WE GOING HOME, I MISS MOM?

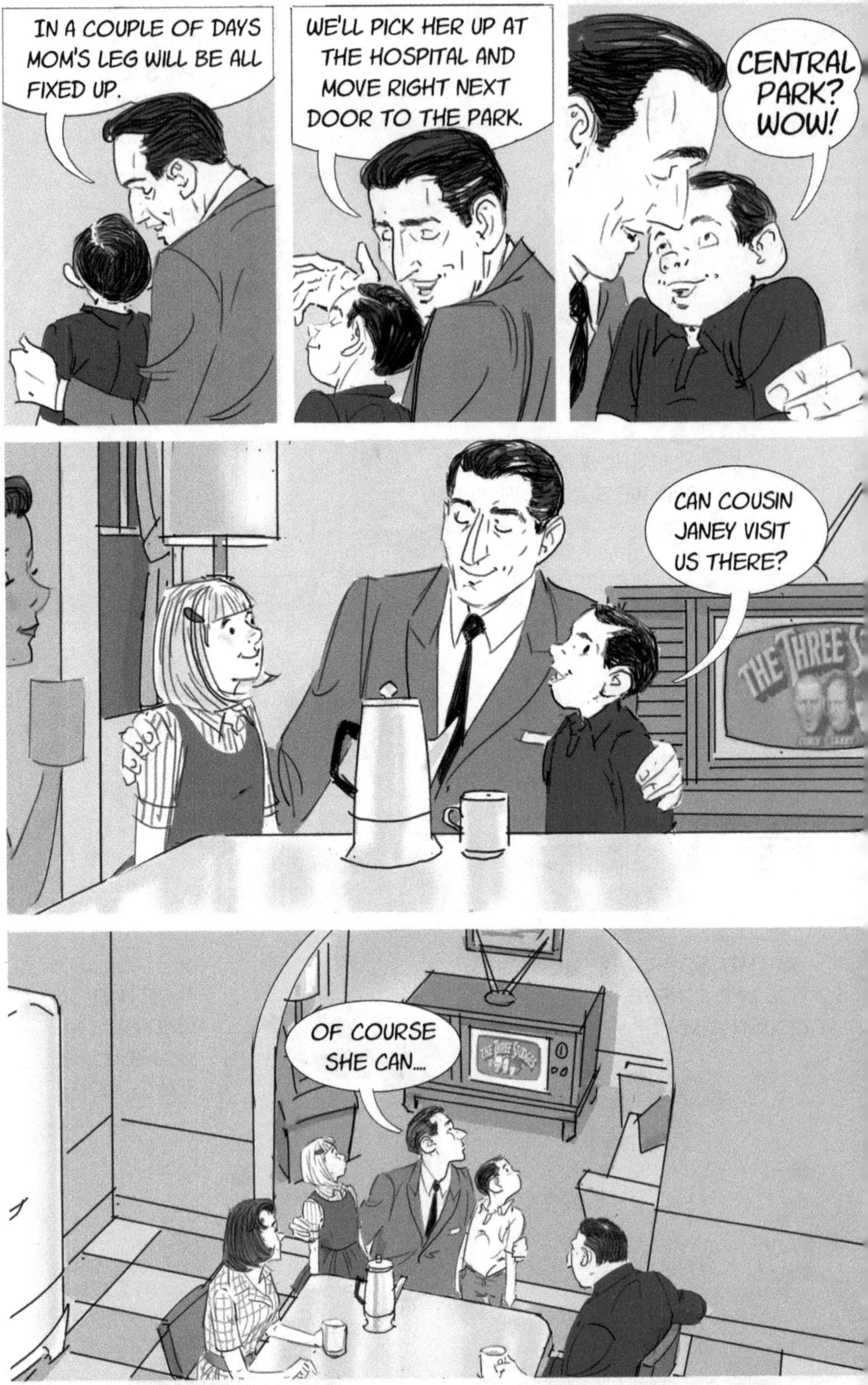
IN A COUPLE OF DAYS MOM'S LEG WILL BE ALL FIXED UP.
WE'LL PICK HER UP AT THE HOSPITAL AND MOVE RIGHT NEXT DOOR TO THE PARK.
CENTRAL PARK? WOW!
CAN COUSIN JANEY VISIT US THERE?
THE THREE S
OF COURSE SHE CAN....
THE THREE STOOGES

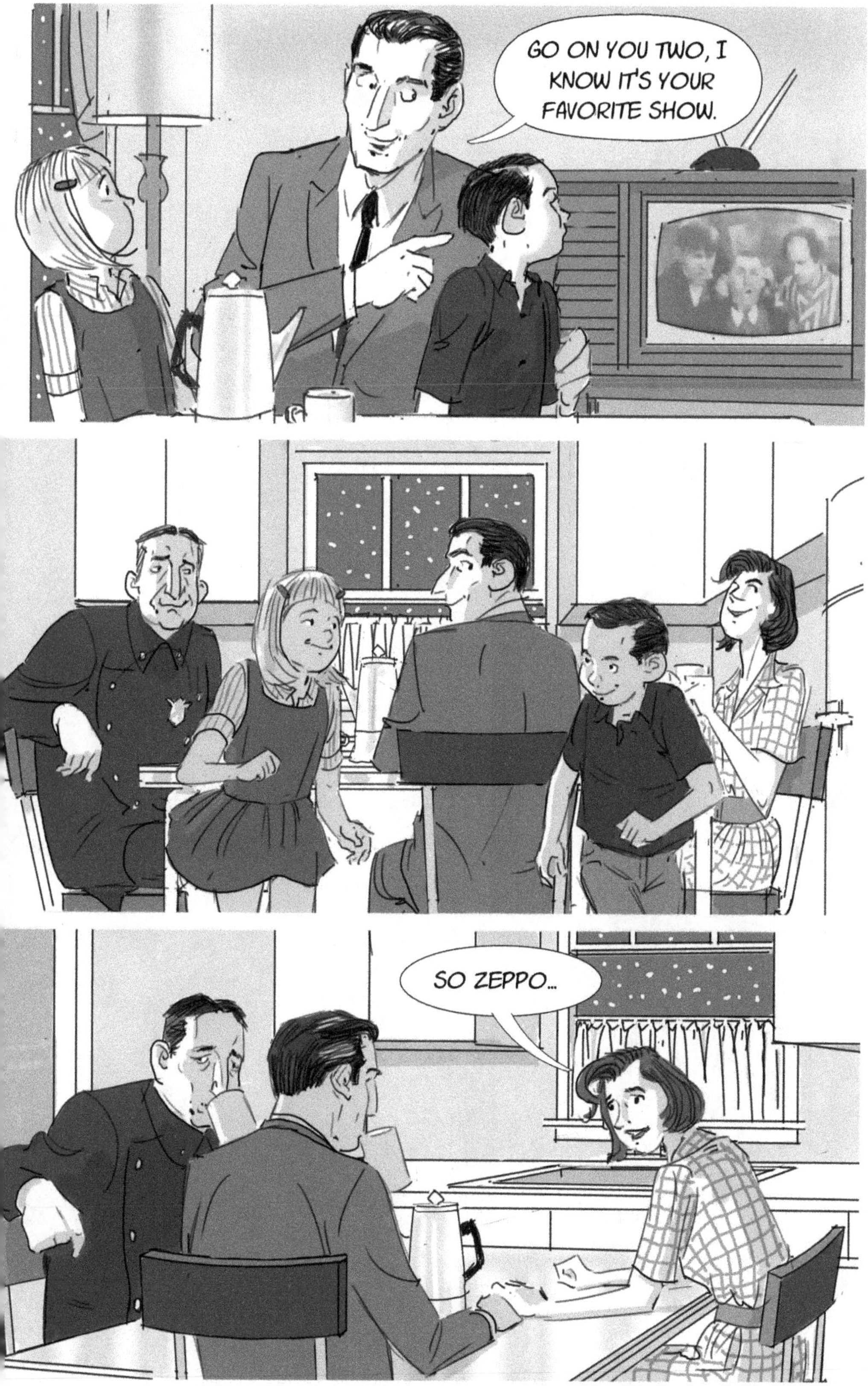
GO ON YOU TWO, I KNOW IT'S YOUR FAVORITE SHOW.
SO ZEPPO...

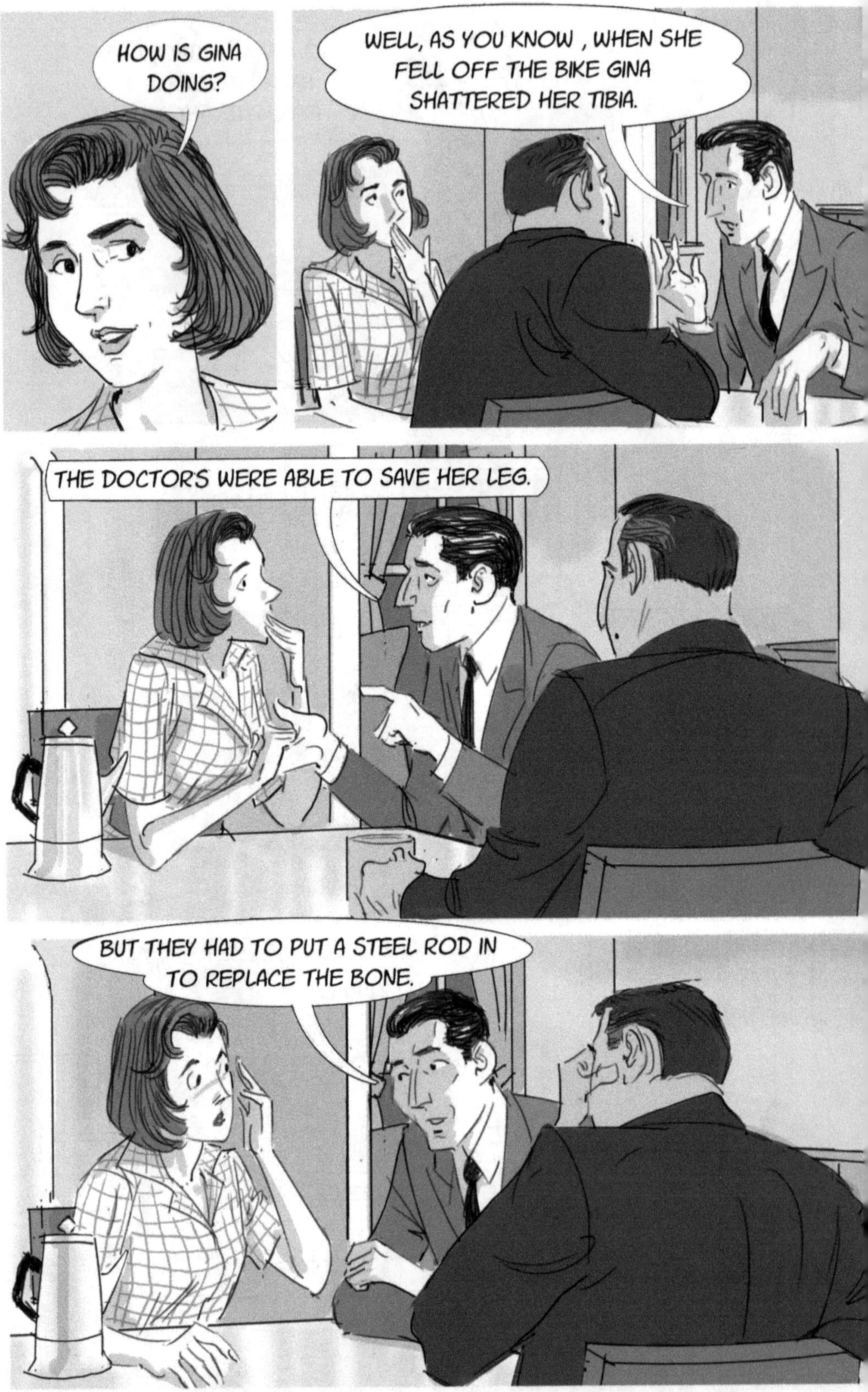
HOW IS GINA DOING?
WELL, AS YOU KNOW , WHEN SHE FELL OFF THE BIKE GINA SHATTERED HER TIBIA.
THE DOCTOR'S WERE ABLE TO SAVE HER LEG.
BUT THEY HAD TO PUT A STEEL ROD IN TO REPLACE THE BONE.

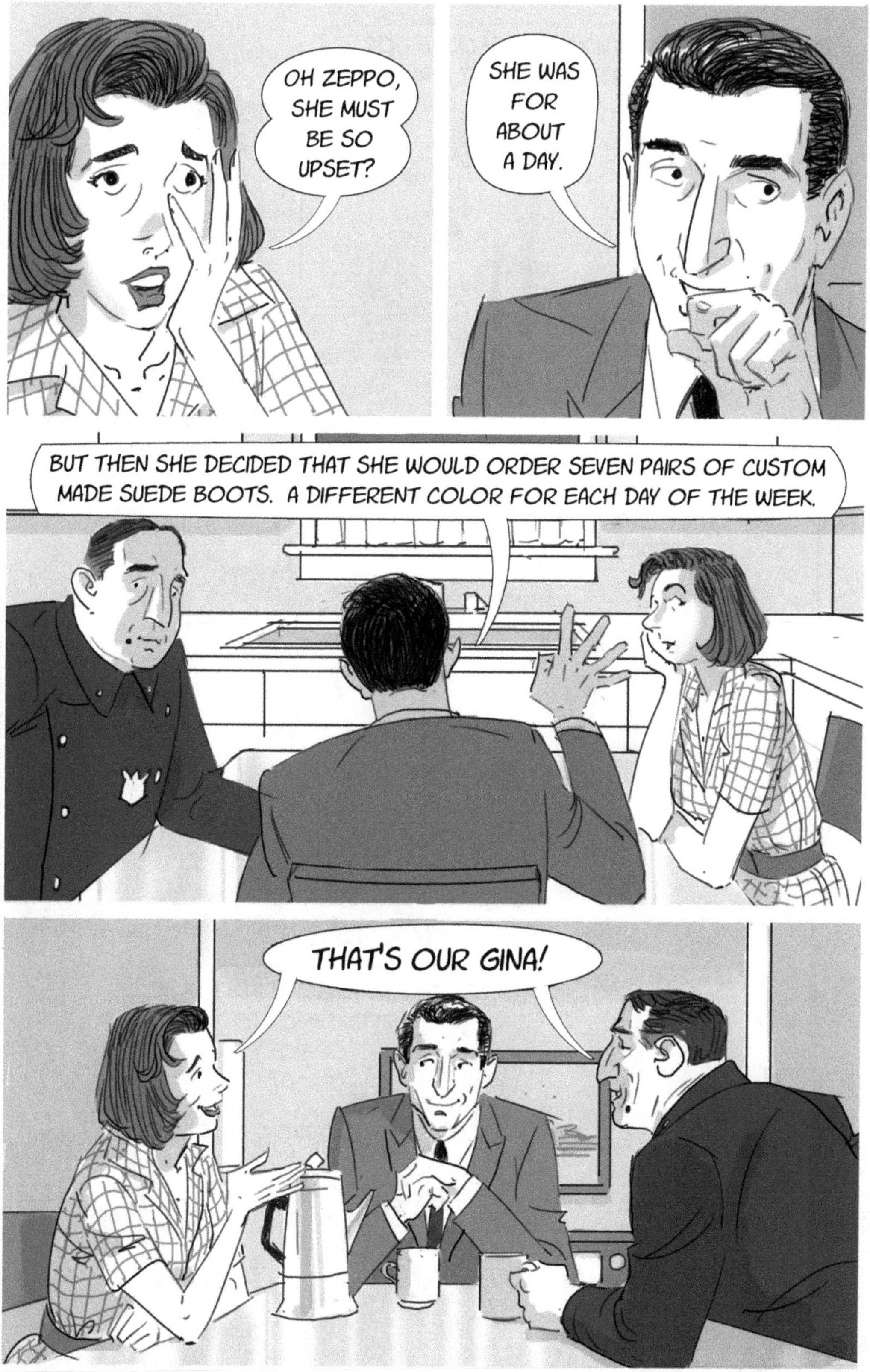
OH ZEPPO, SHE MUST BE SO UPSET?
SHE WAS FOR ABOUT A DAY.
BUT THEN SHE DECIDED THAT SHE WOULD ORDER SEVEN PAIRS OF CUSTOM MADE SUEDE BOOTS. A DIFFERENT COLOR FOR EACH DAY OF THE WEEK.
THAT'S OUR GINA!

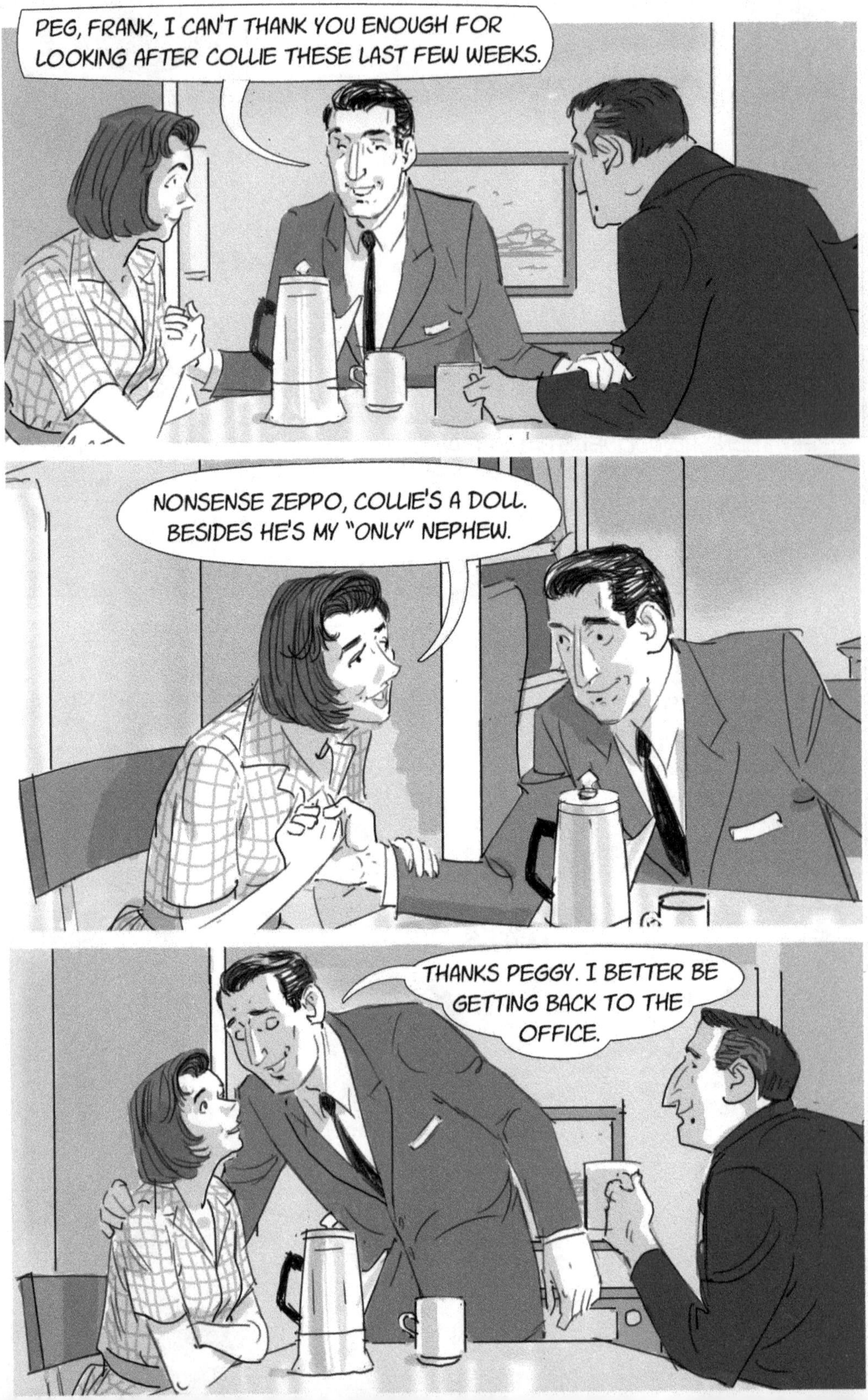
PEG, FRANK, I CAN'T THANK YOU ENOUGH FOR LOOKING AFTER COLLIE THESE LAST FEW WEEKS.
NONSENSE ZEPPO, COLLIE'S A DOLL. BESIDES HE'S MY "ONLY" NEPHEW.
THANKS PEGGY. I BETTER BE GETTING BACK TO THE OFFICE.

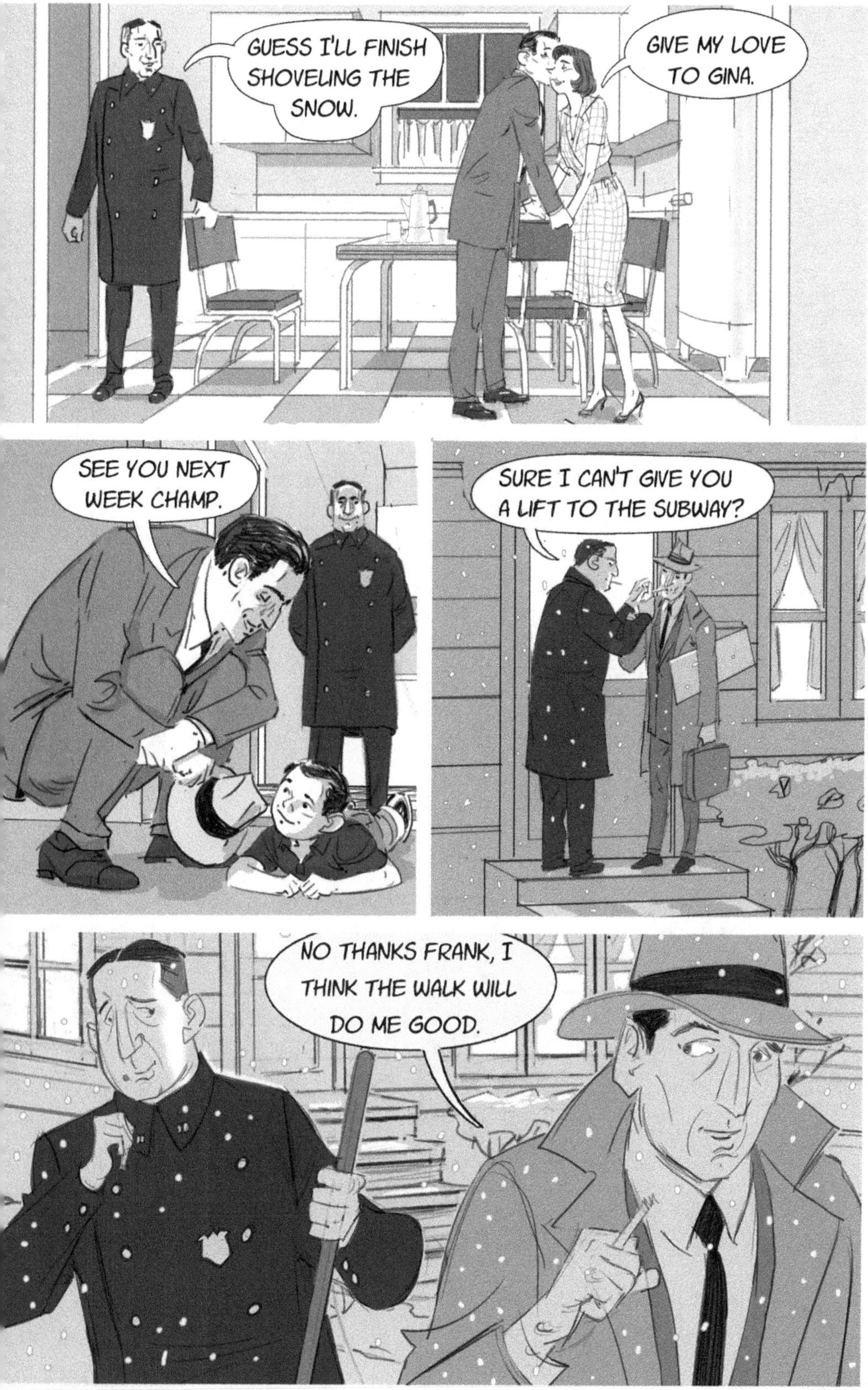
GUESS I'LL FINISH SHOVELING THE SNOW.
GIVE MY LOVE TO GINA.
SEE YOU NEXT WEEK CHAMP.
SURE I CAN'T GIVE YOU A LIFT TO THE SUBWAY?
NO THANKS FRANK, I THINK THE WALK WILL DO ME GOOD.

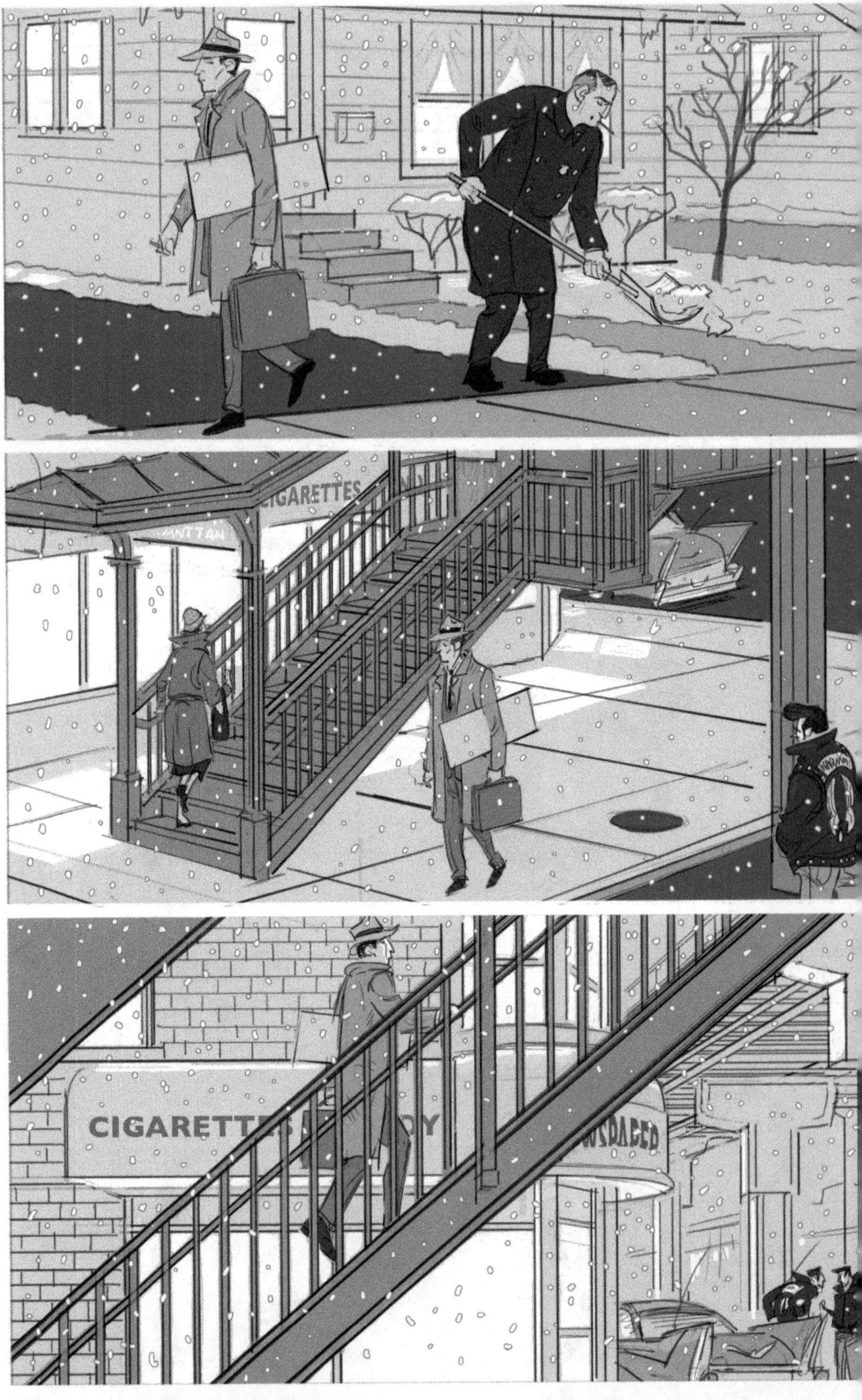
CIGARETTES
CIGARETTES

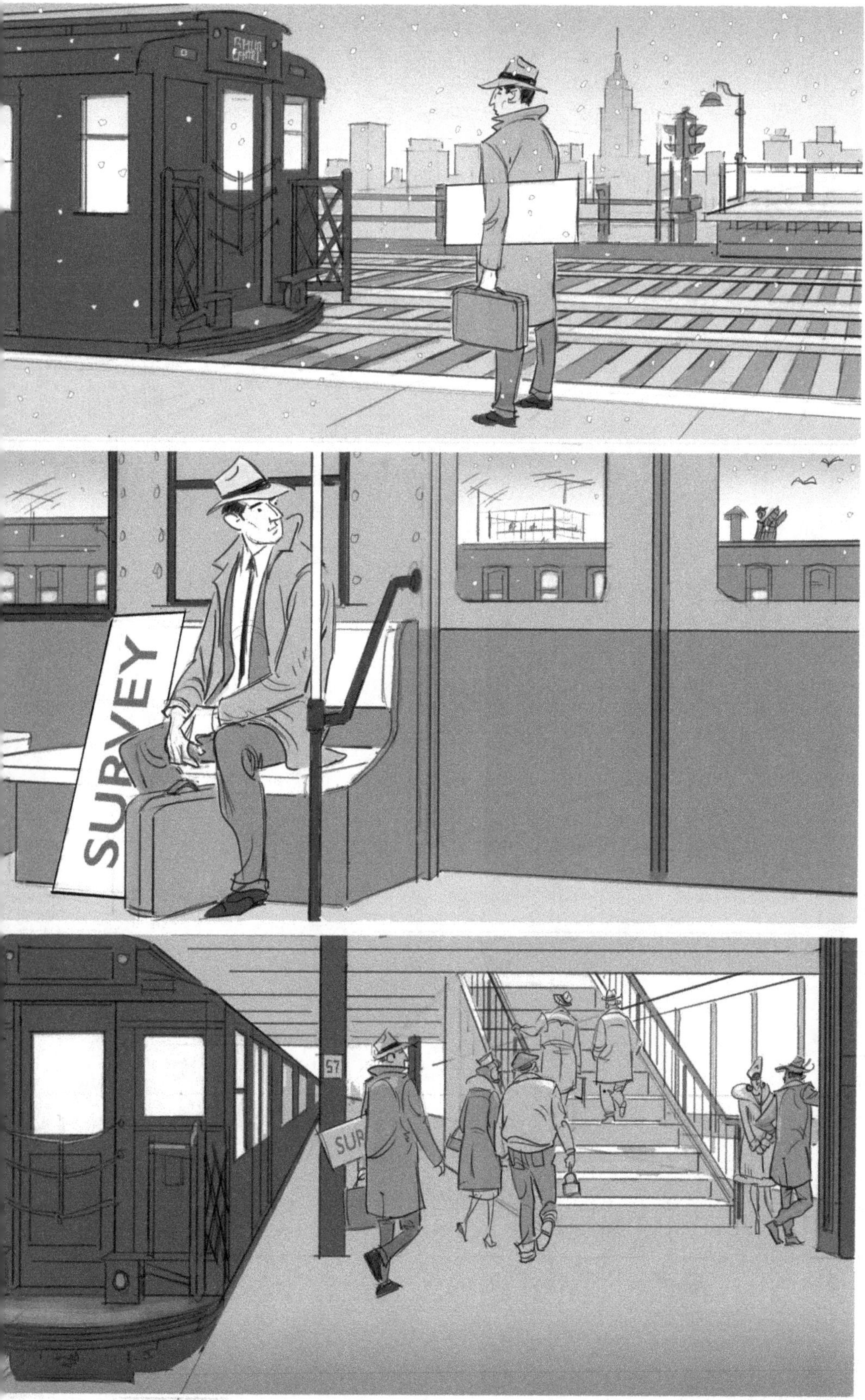
SURVEY
57
SUR

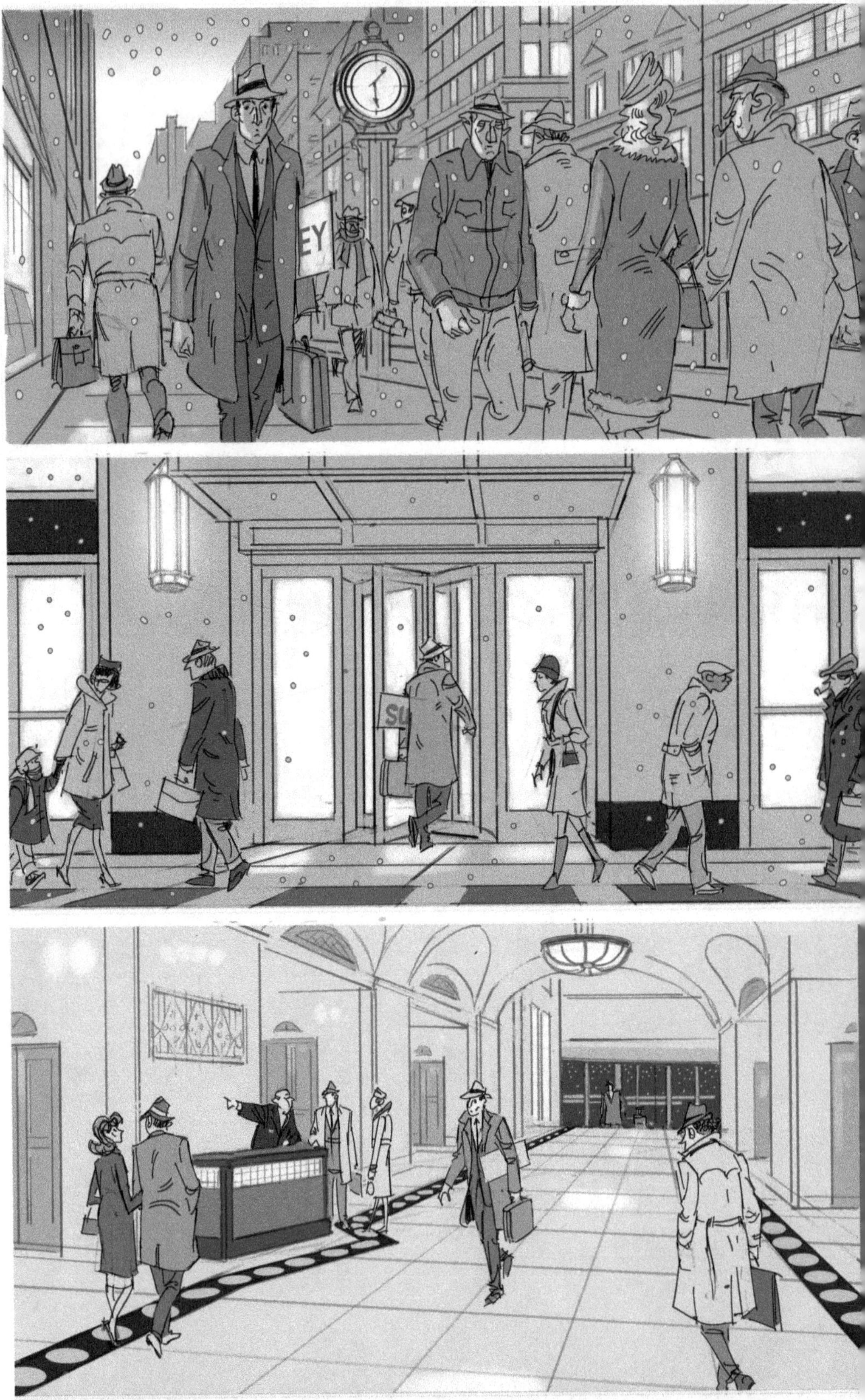

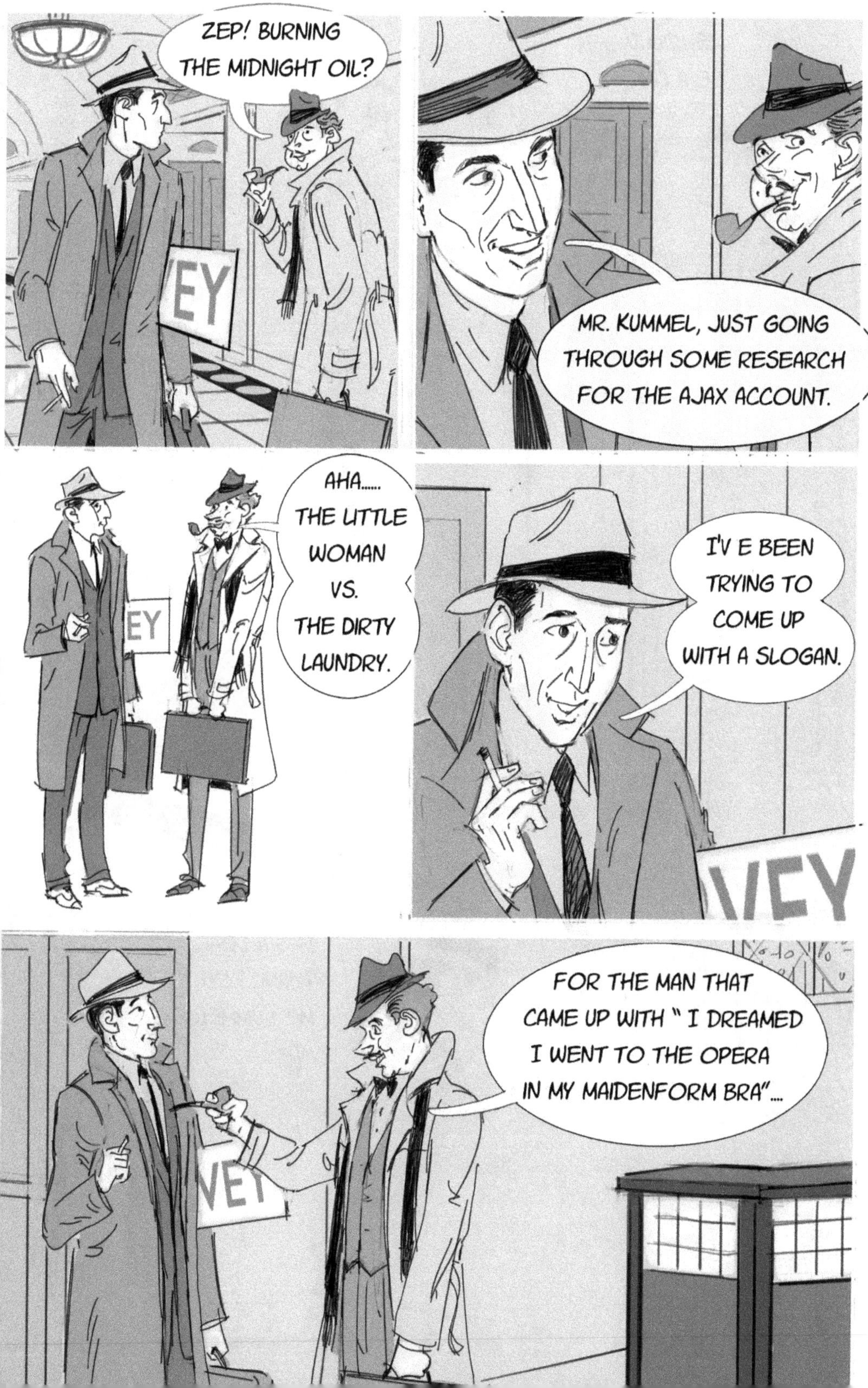
ZEP! BURNING THE MIDNIGHT OIL?
EY
MR. KUMMEL, JUST GOING THROUGH SOME RESEARCH FOR THE AJAX ACCOUNT.
AHA...... THE LITTLE WOMAN VS. THE DIRTY LAUNDRY.
EY
I'V E BEEN TRYING TO COME UP WITH A SLOGAN.
VEY
FOR THE MAN THAT CAME UP WITH " I DREAMED I WENT TO THE OPERA IN MY MAIDENFORM BRA"....
VEY

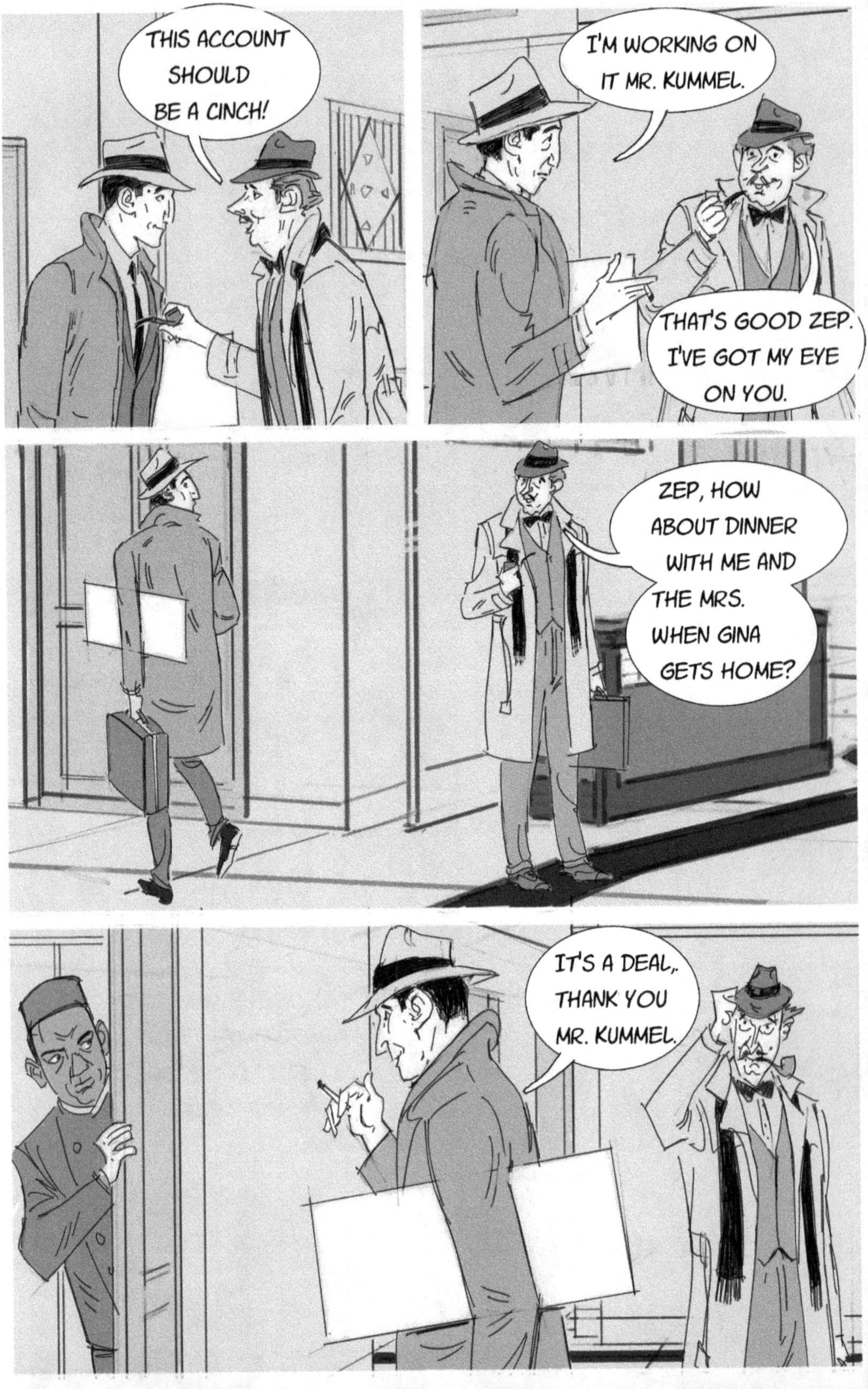
THIS ACCOUNT SHOULD BE A CINCH!
I'M WORKING ON IT MR. KUMMEL.
THAT'S GOOD ZEP. I'VE GOT MY EYE ON YOU.
ZEP, HOW ABOUT DINNER WITH ME AND THE MRS. WHEN GINA GETS HOME?
IT'S A DEAL,. THANK YOU MR. KUMMEL.

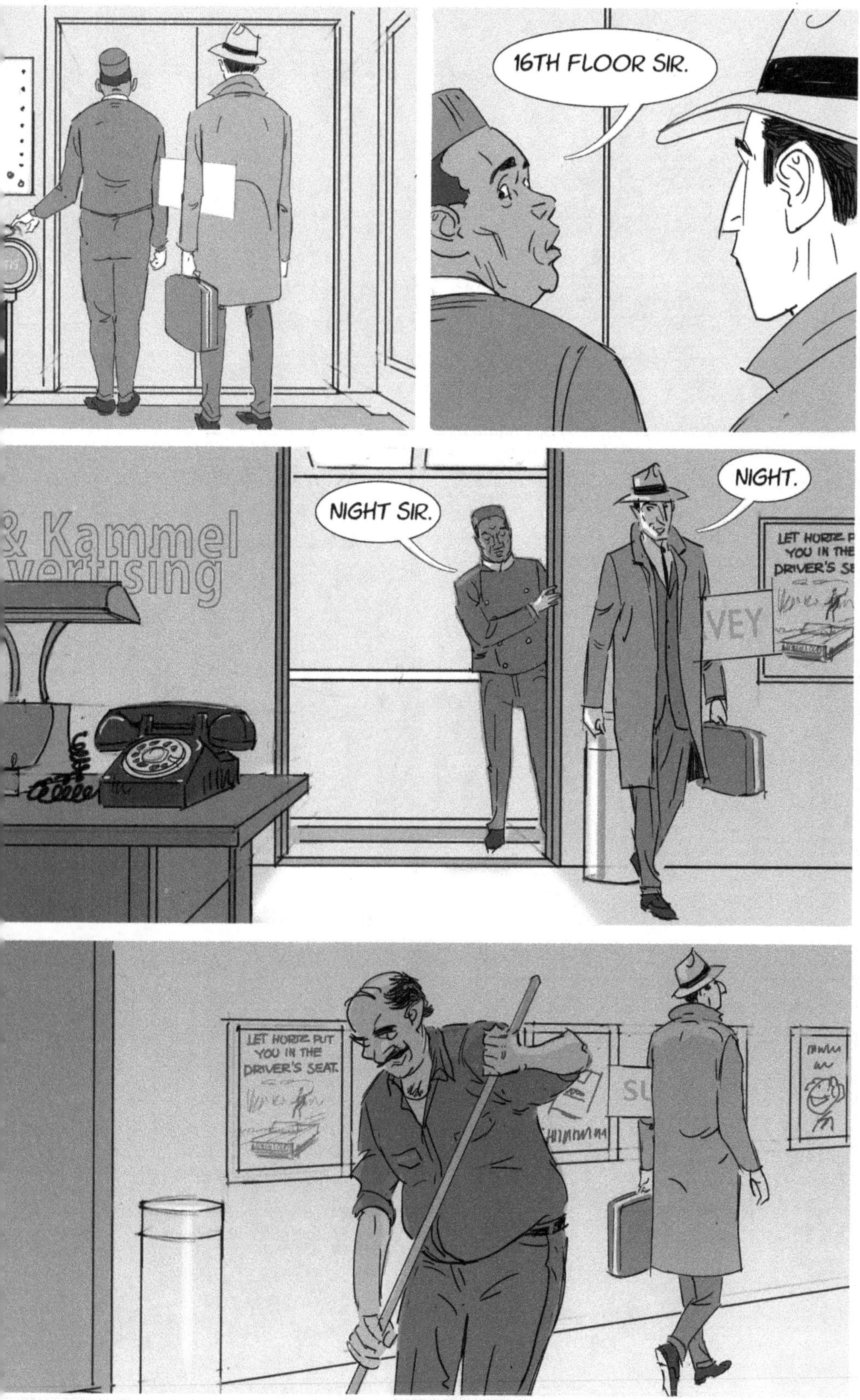
16TH FLOOR SIR.
& Kammel
vertising
NIGHT SIR.
NIGHT.
LET HORTZ PUT YOU IN THE DRIVER'S SEAT.

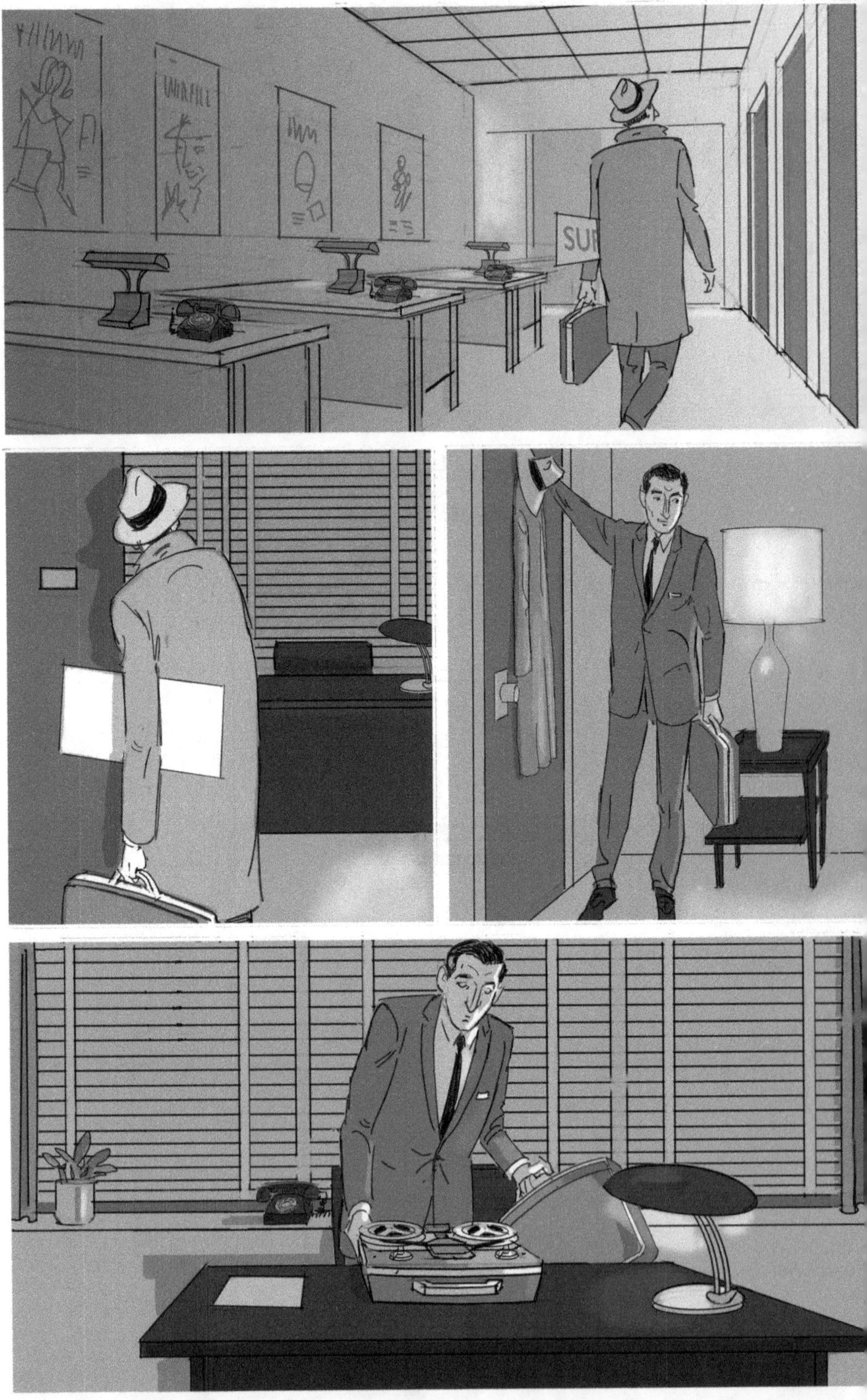

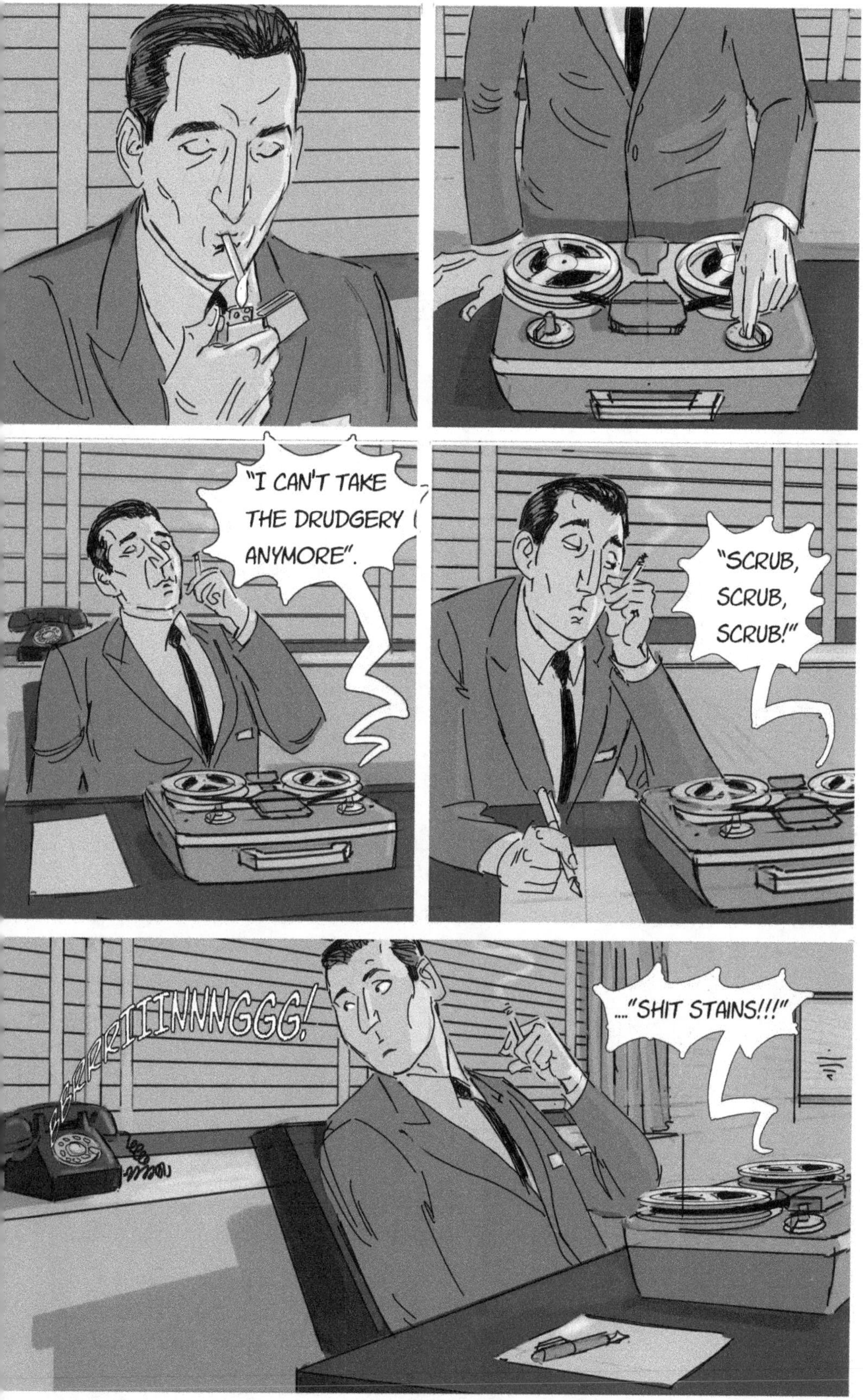
"I CAN'T TAKE THE DRUDGERY ANYMORE".
"SCRUB, SCRUB, SCRUB!"
BRRRIIIINNNGGG!
..."SHIT STAINS!!!"

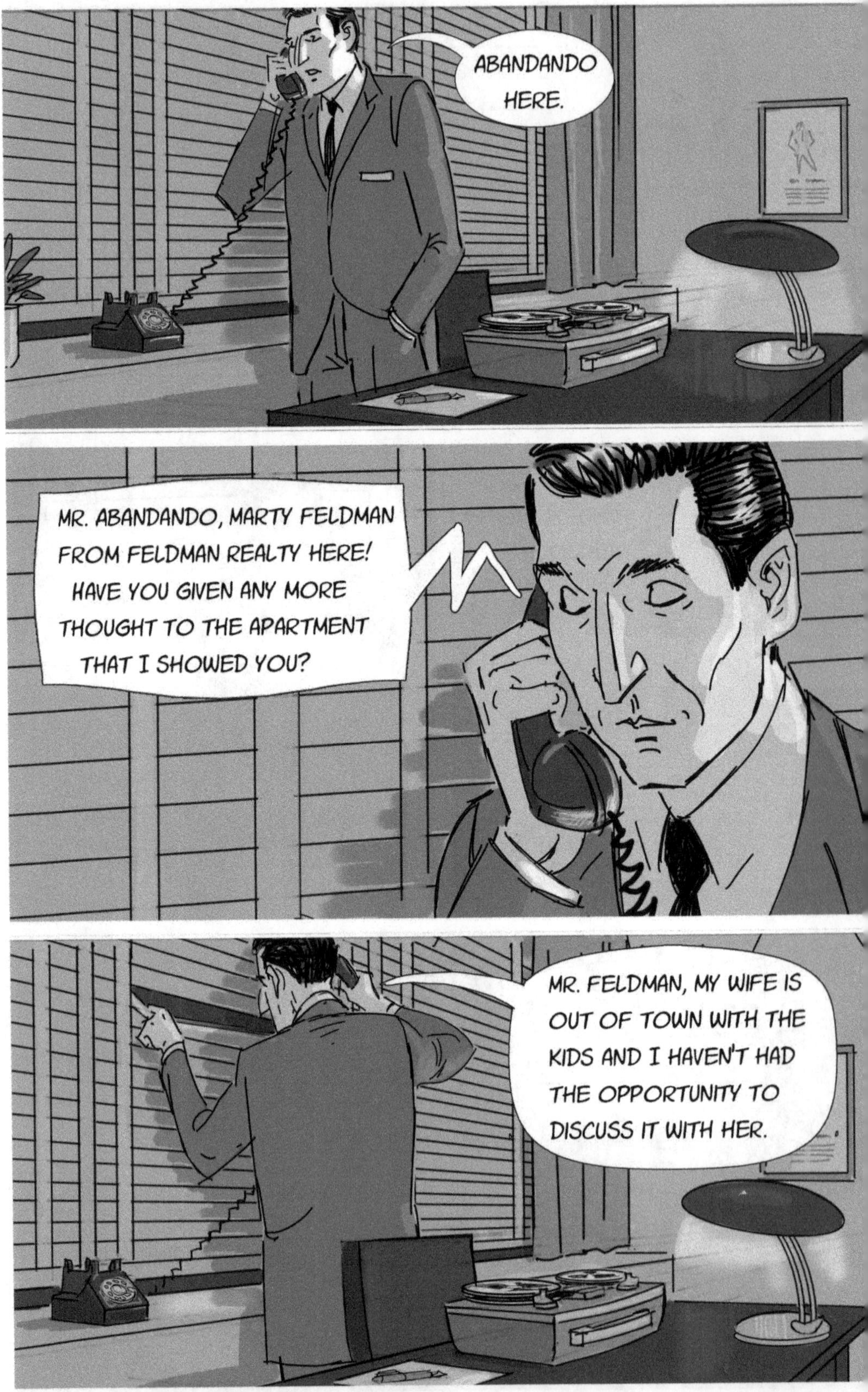
ABANDANDO HERE.
MR. ABANDANDO, MARTY FELDMAN FROM FELDMAN REALTY HERE! HAVE YOU GIVEN ANY MORE THOUGHT TO THE APARTMENT THAT I SHOWED YOU?
MR. FELDMAN, MY WIFE IS OUT OF TOWN WITH THE KIDS AND I HAVEN'T HAD THE OPPORTUNITY TO DISCUSS IT WITH HER.

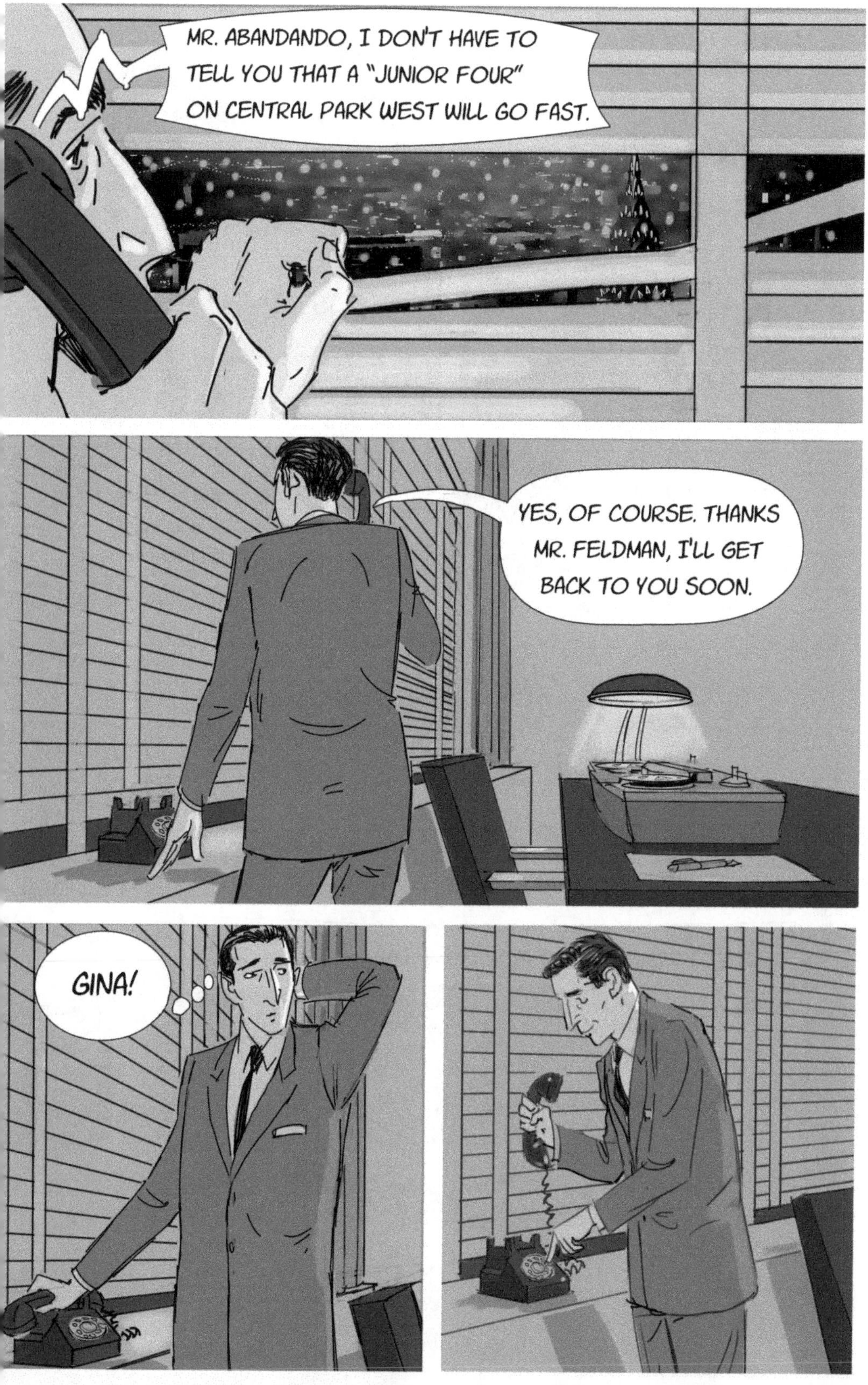
MR. ABANDANDO, I DON'T HAVE TO TELL YOU THAT A "JUNIOR FOUR" ON CENTRAL PARK WEST WILL GO FAST.
YES, OF COURSE. THANKS MR. FELDMAN, I'LL GET BACK TO YOU SOON.
GINA!

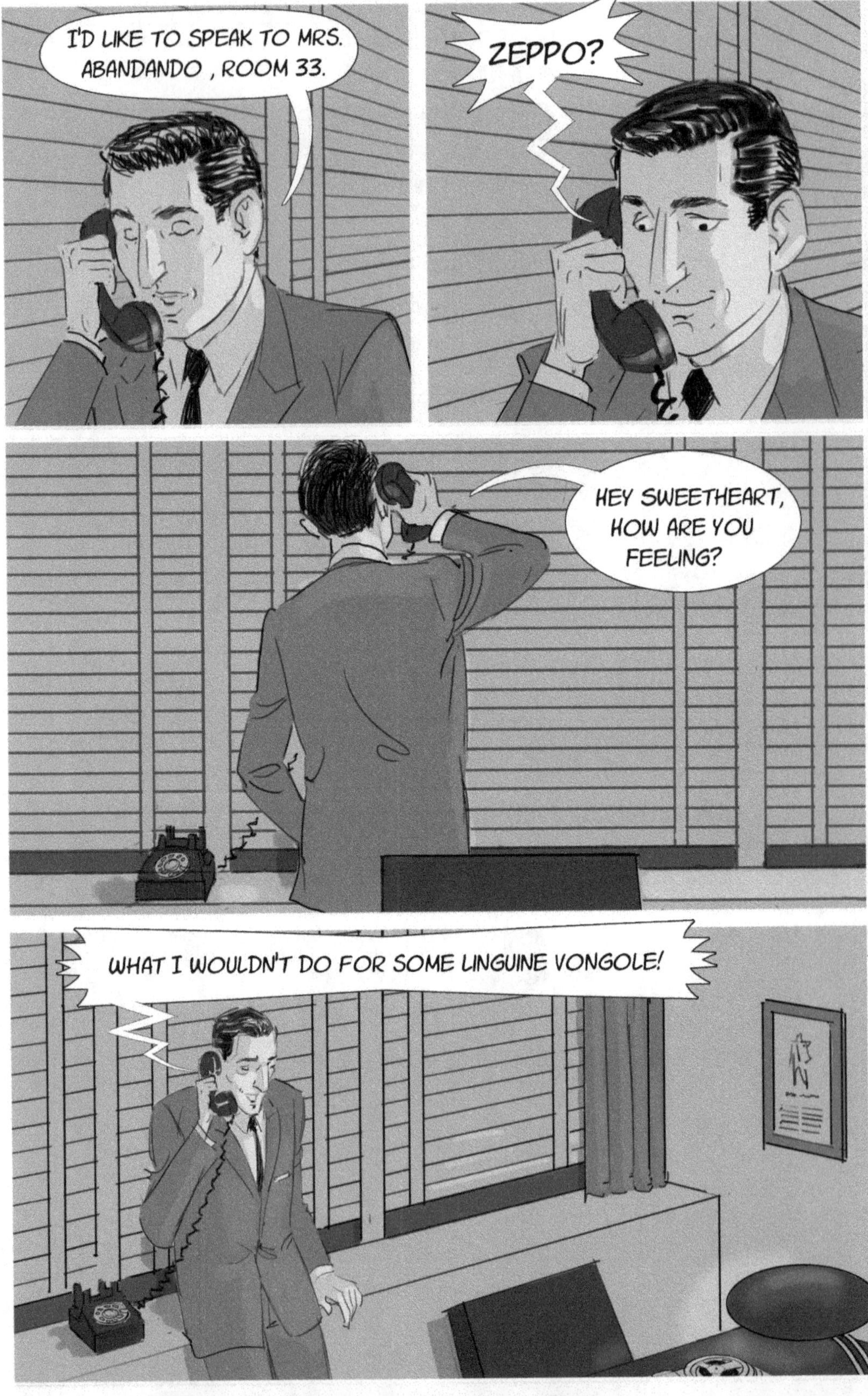
I'D LIKE TO SPEAK TO MRS. ABANDANDO , ROOM 33.
ZEPPO?
HEY SWEETHEART, HOW ARE YOU FEELING?
WHAT I WOULDN'T DO FOR SOME LINGUINE VONGOLE!

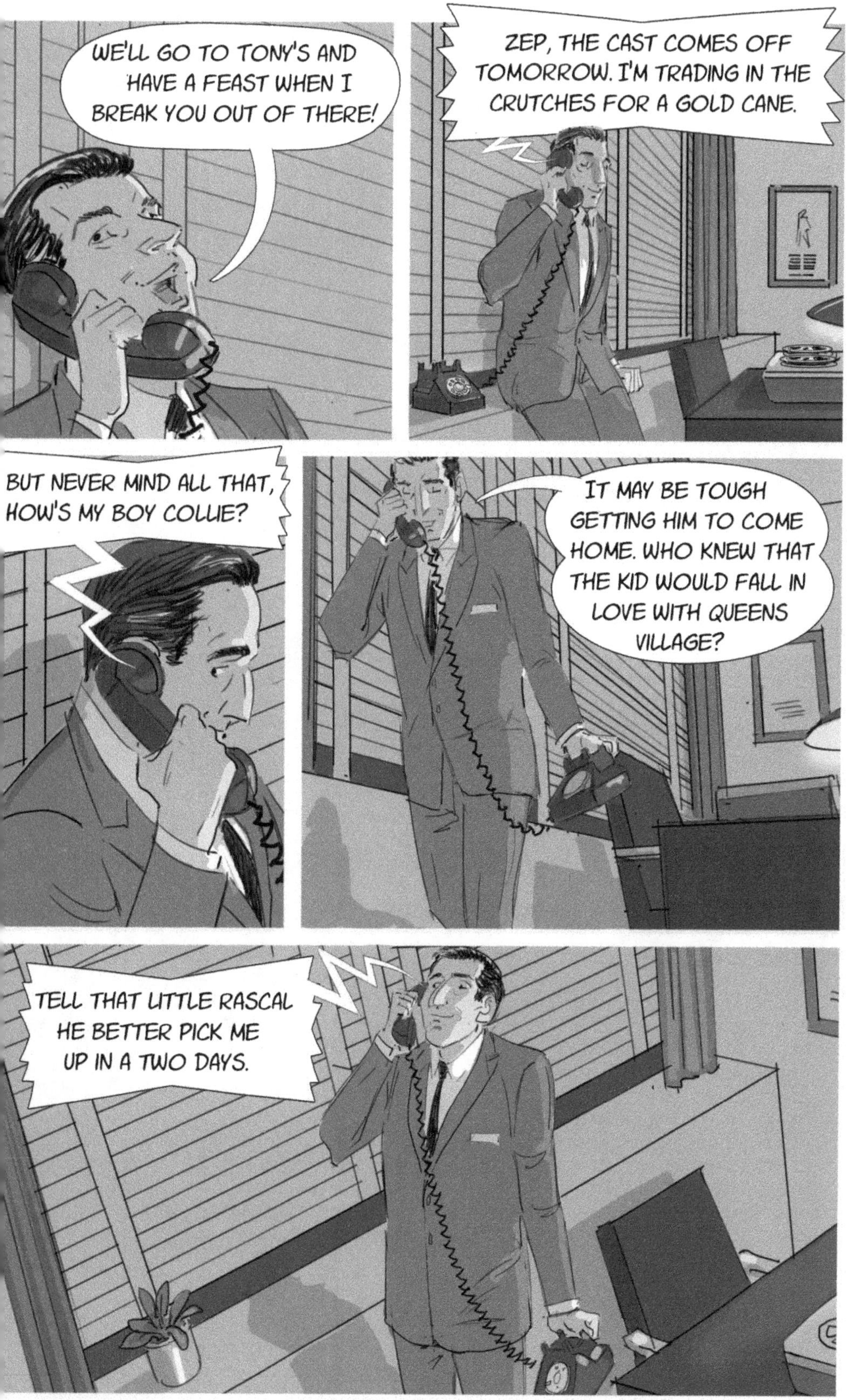
WE'LL GO TO TONY'S AND HAVE A FEAST WHEN I BREAK YOU OUT OF THERE!
ZEP, THE CAST COMES OFF TOMORROW. I'M TRADING IN THE CRUTCHES FOR A GOLD CANE.
BUT NEVER MIND ALL THAT, HOW'S MY BOY COLLIE?
IT MAY BE TOUGH GETTING HIM TO COME HOME. WHO KNEW THAT THE KID WOULD FALL IN LOVE WITH QUEENS VILLAGE?
TELL THAT LITTLE RASCAL HE BETTER PICK ME UP IN A TWO DAYS.

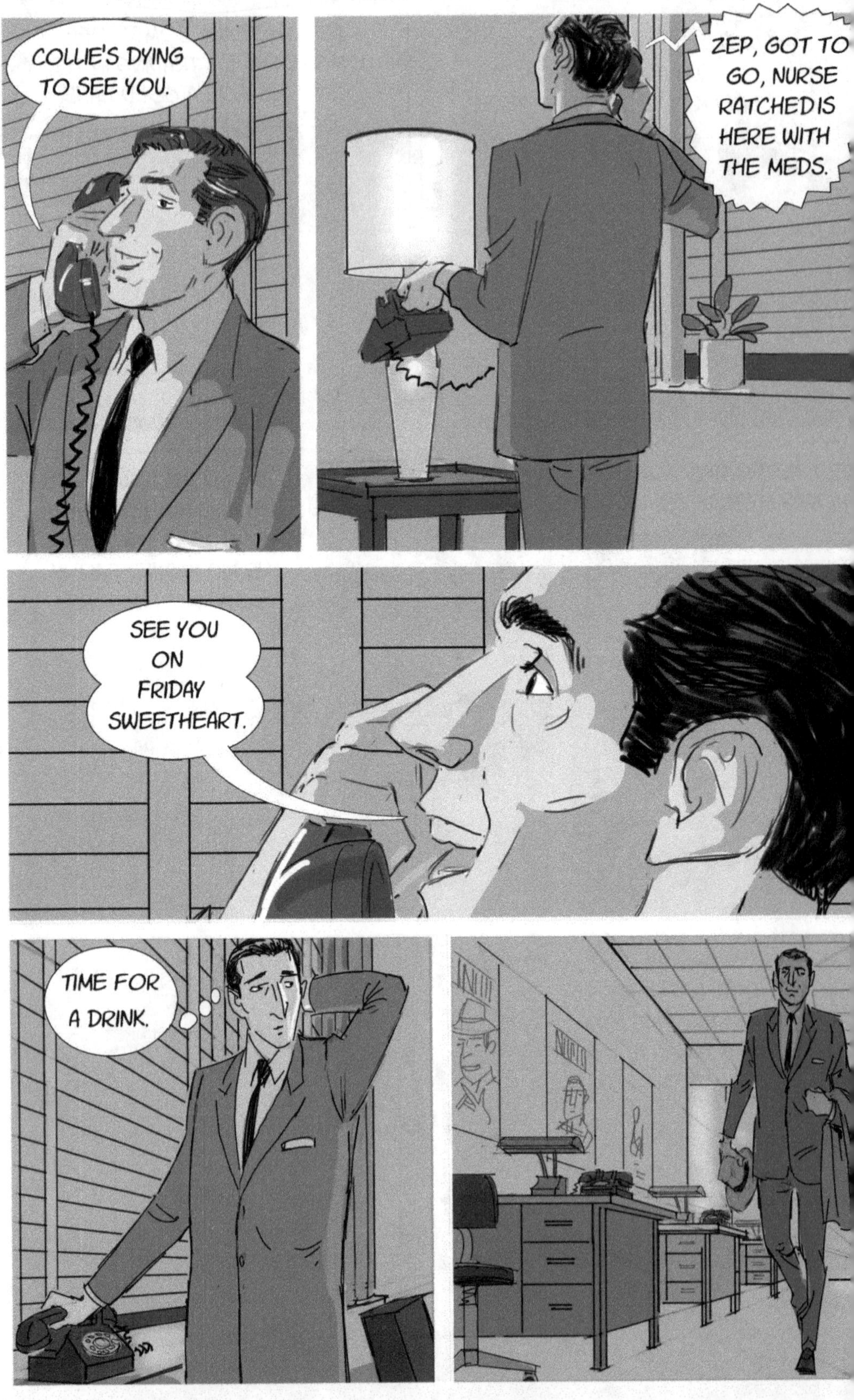
COLLIE'S DYING TO SEE YOU.
ZEP, GOT TO GO, NURSE RATCHED IS HERE WITH THE MEDS.
SEE YOU ON FRIDAY SWEETHEART.
TIME FOR A DRINK.

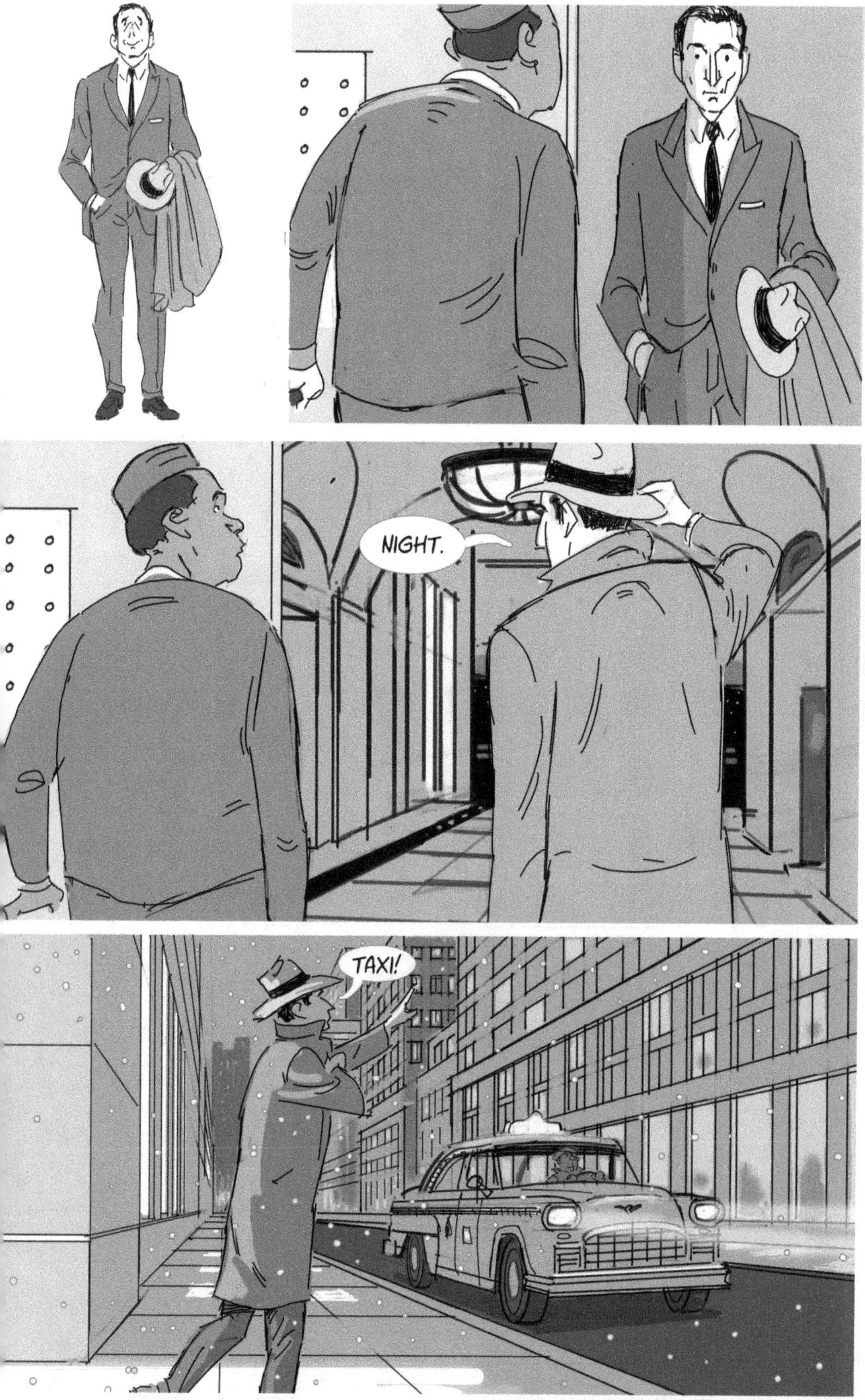
NIGHT.
TAXI!

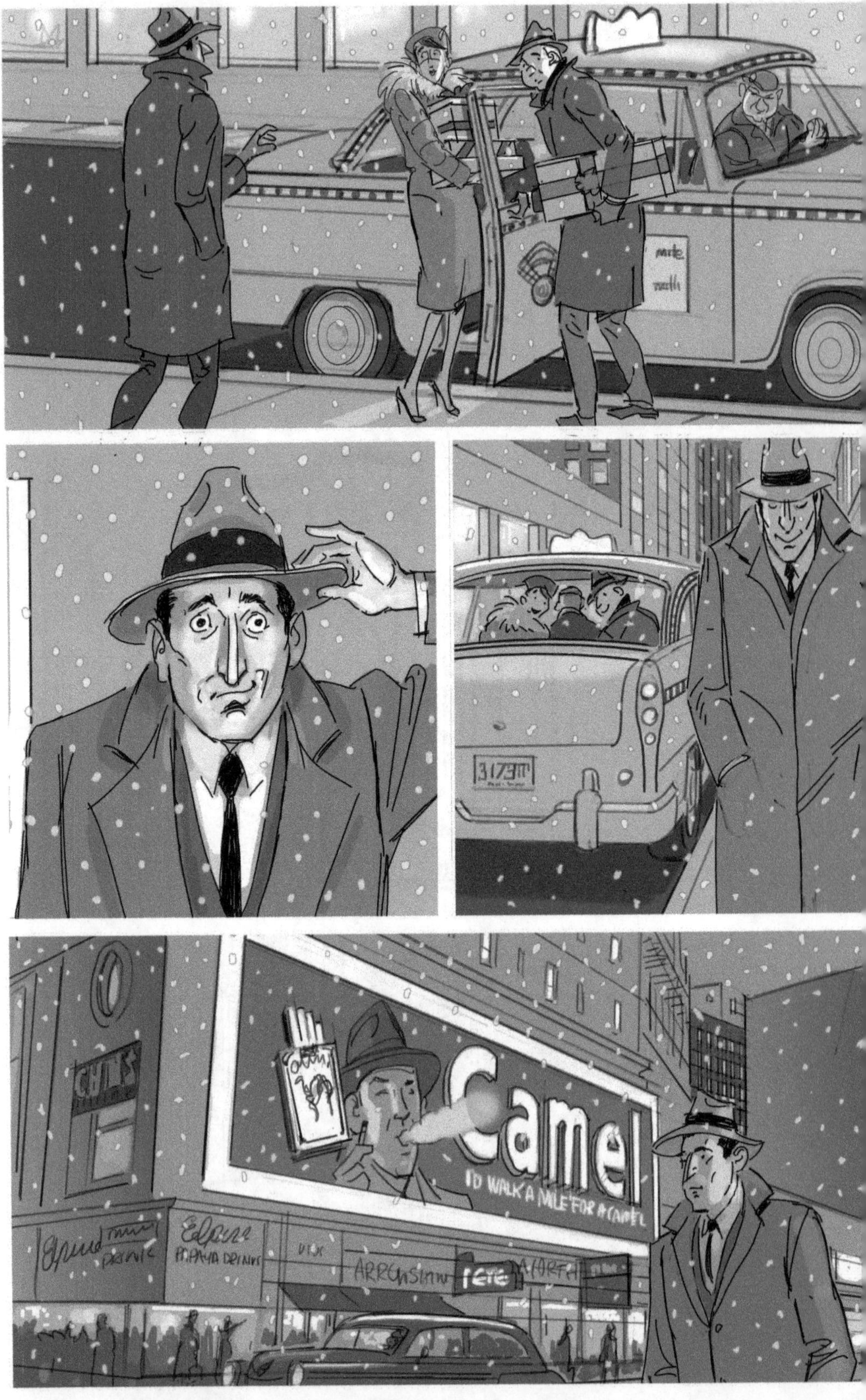

Camel
I'D WALK A MILE FOR A CAMEL

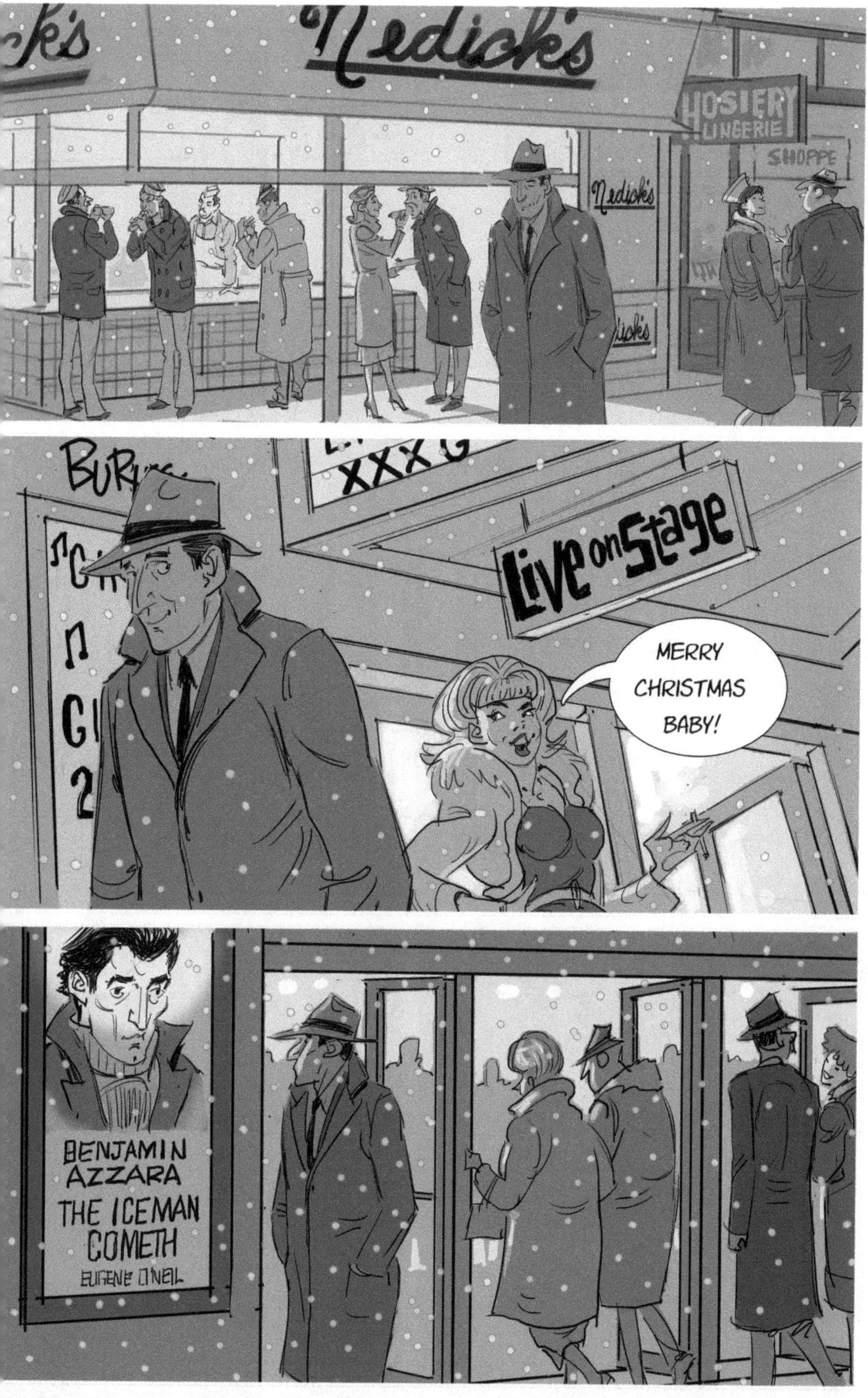
Nedick's
HOSIERY
LINGERIE
SHOPPE
Nedick's
Live on Stage
MERRY CHRISTMAS BABY!
BENJAMIN AZZARA
THE ICEMAN COMETH
EUGENE O'NEIL

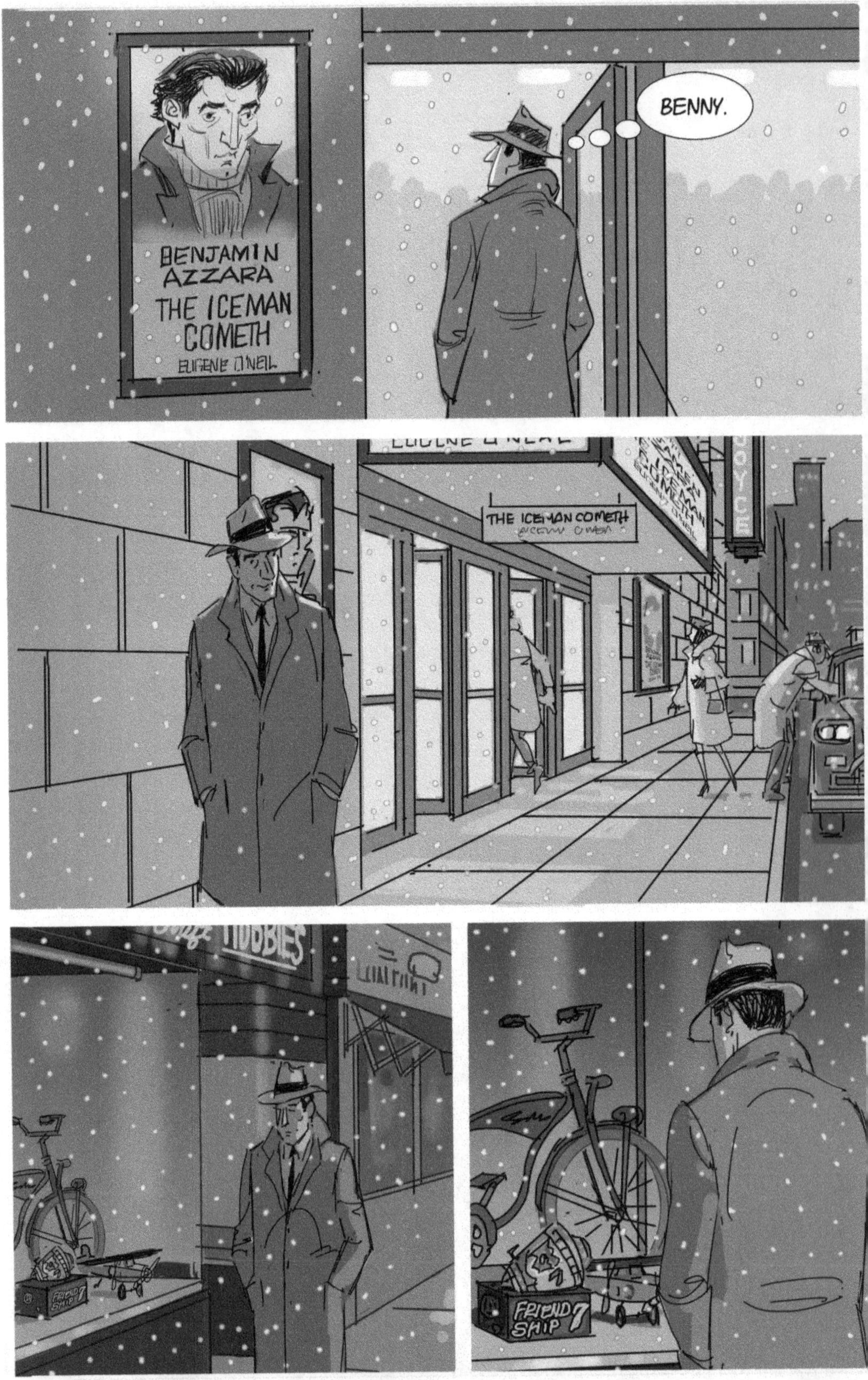
BENJAMIN AZZARA
THE ICEMAN COMETH
EUGENE O'NEIL
BENNY.
THE ICEMAN COMETH
JOYCE
HOBBIES
FRIEND SHIP 7

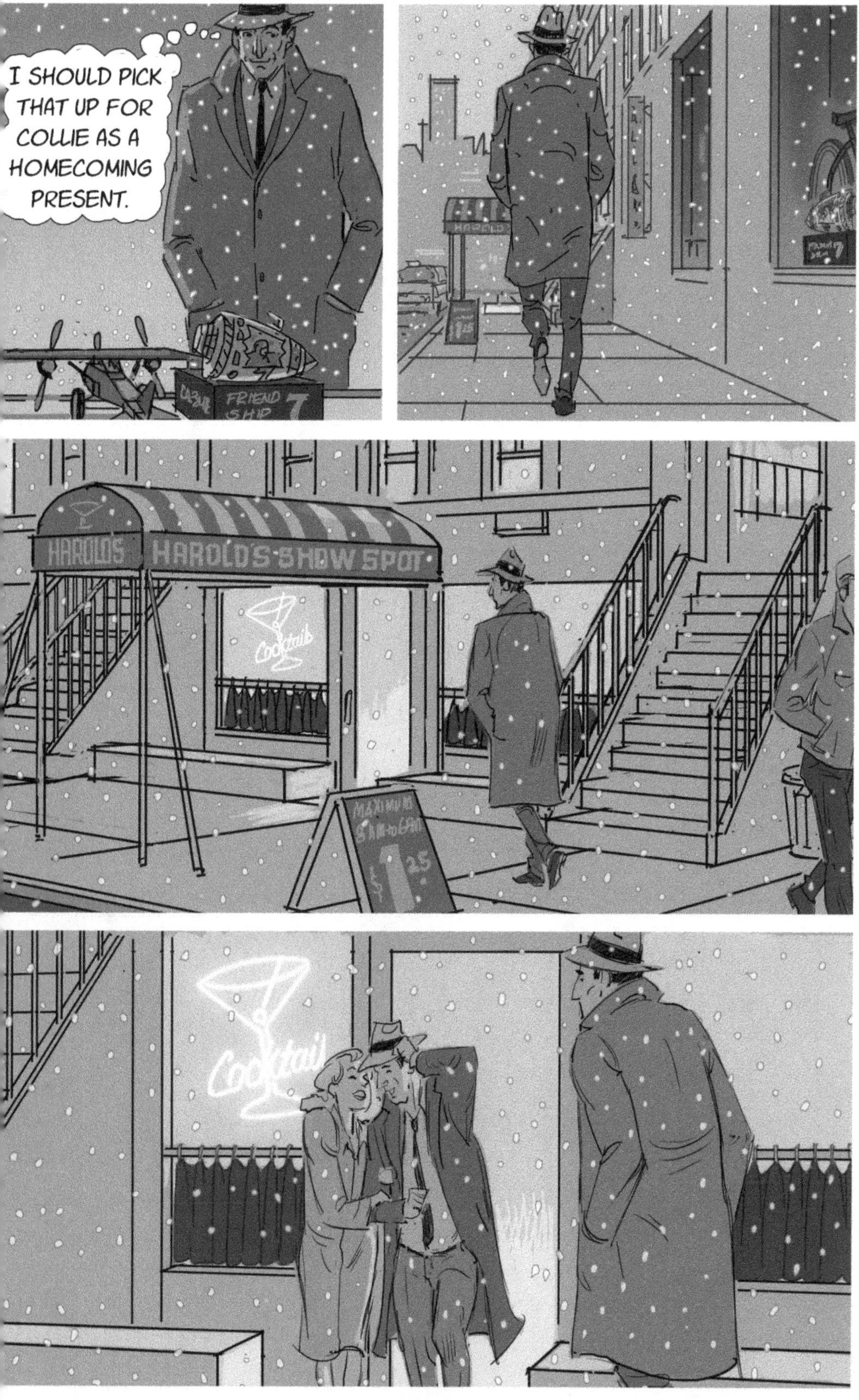
I SHOULD PICK THAT UP FOR COLLIE AS A HOMECOMING PRESENT.
FRIEND SHIP 7
HAROLDS
HAROLD'S SHOW SPOT
Cocktail

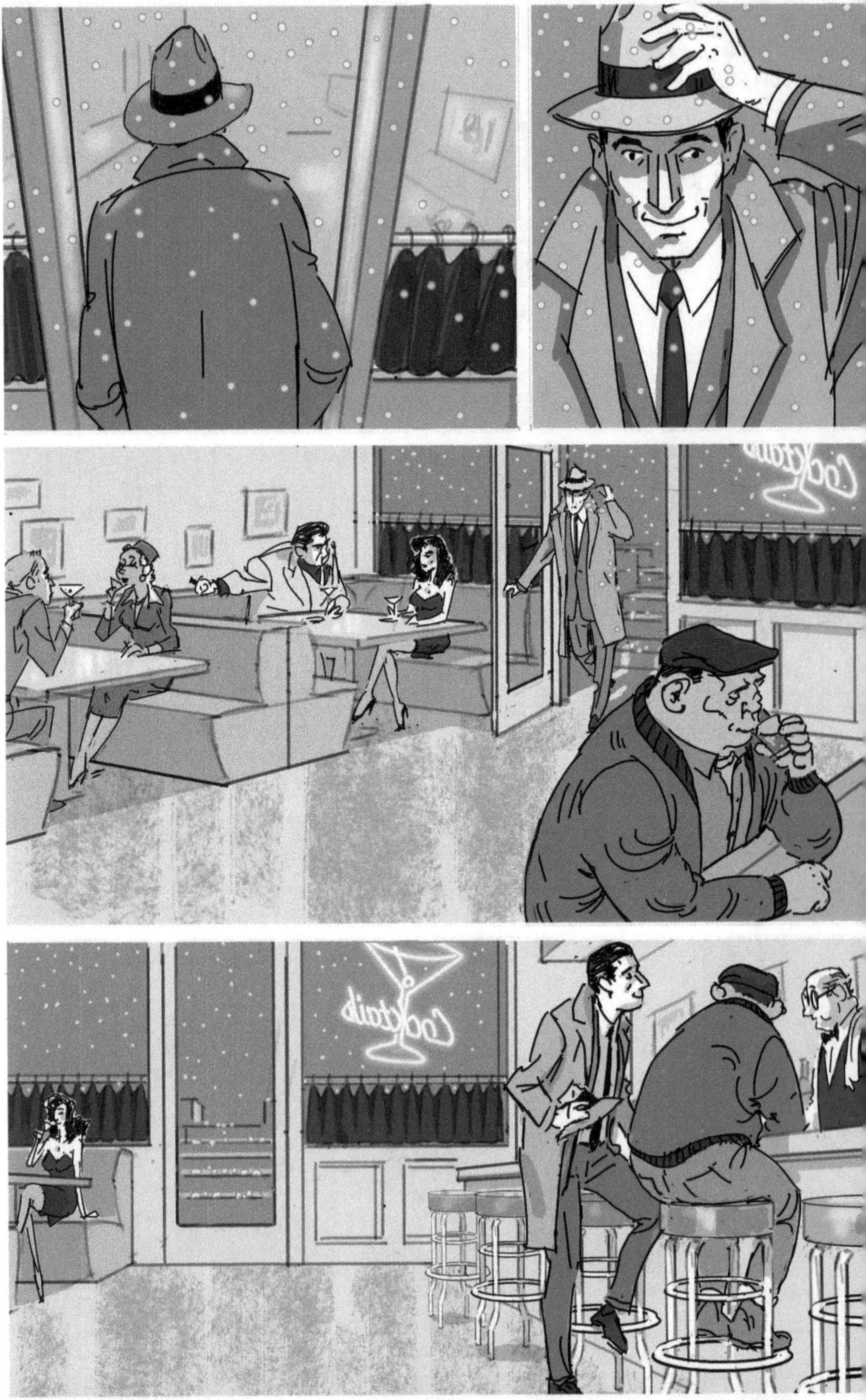

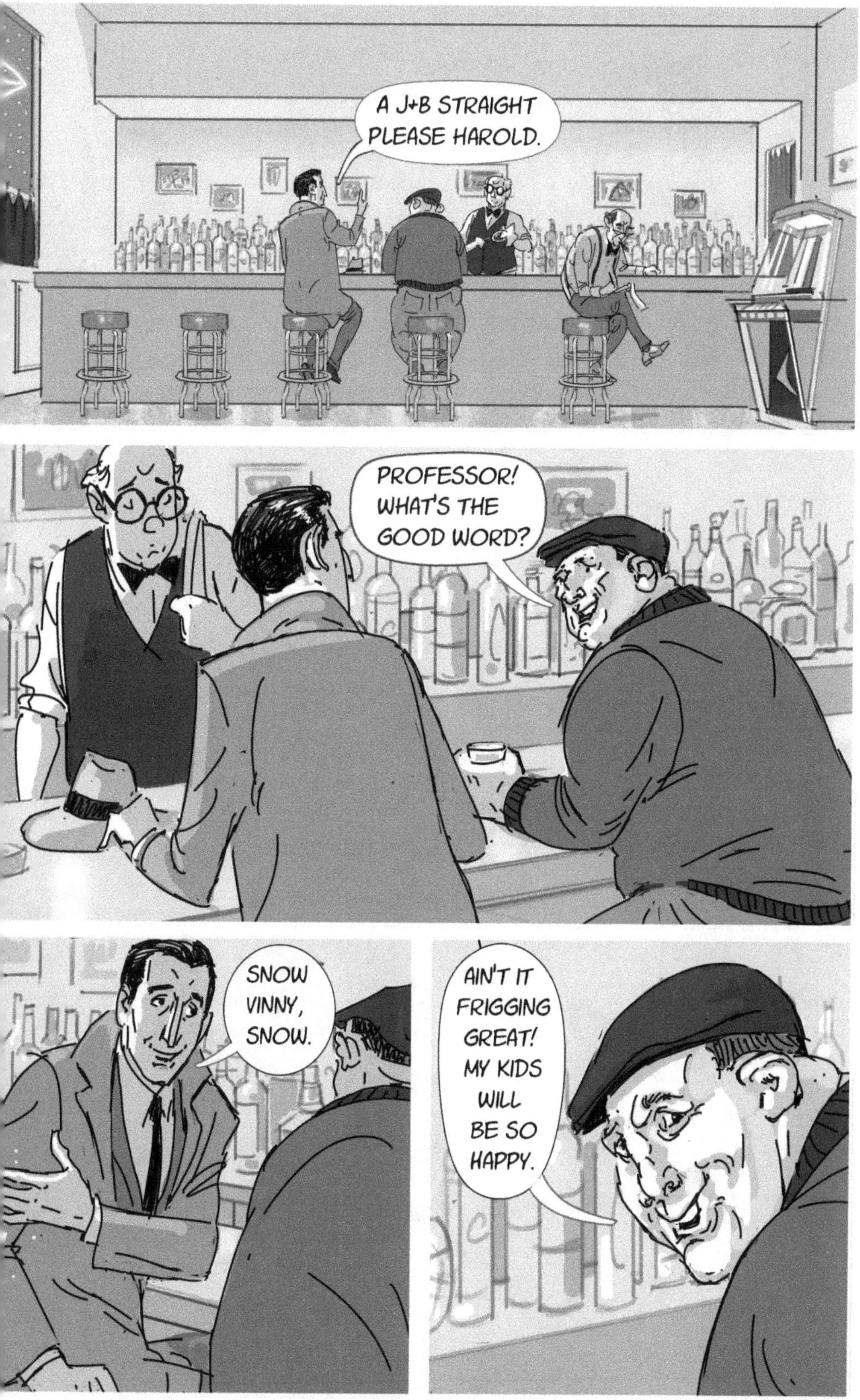
A J+B STRAIGHT PLEASE HAROLD.
PROFESSOR! WHAT'S THE GOOD WORD?
SNOW VINNY, SNOW.
AIN'T IT FRIGGING GREAT! MY KIDS WILL BE SO HAPPY.

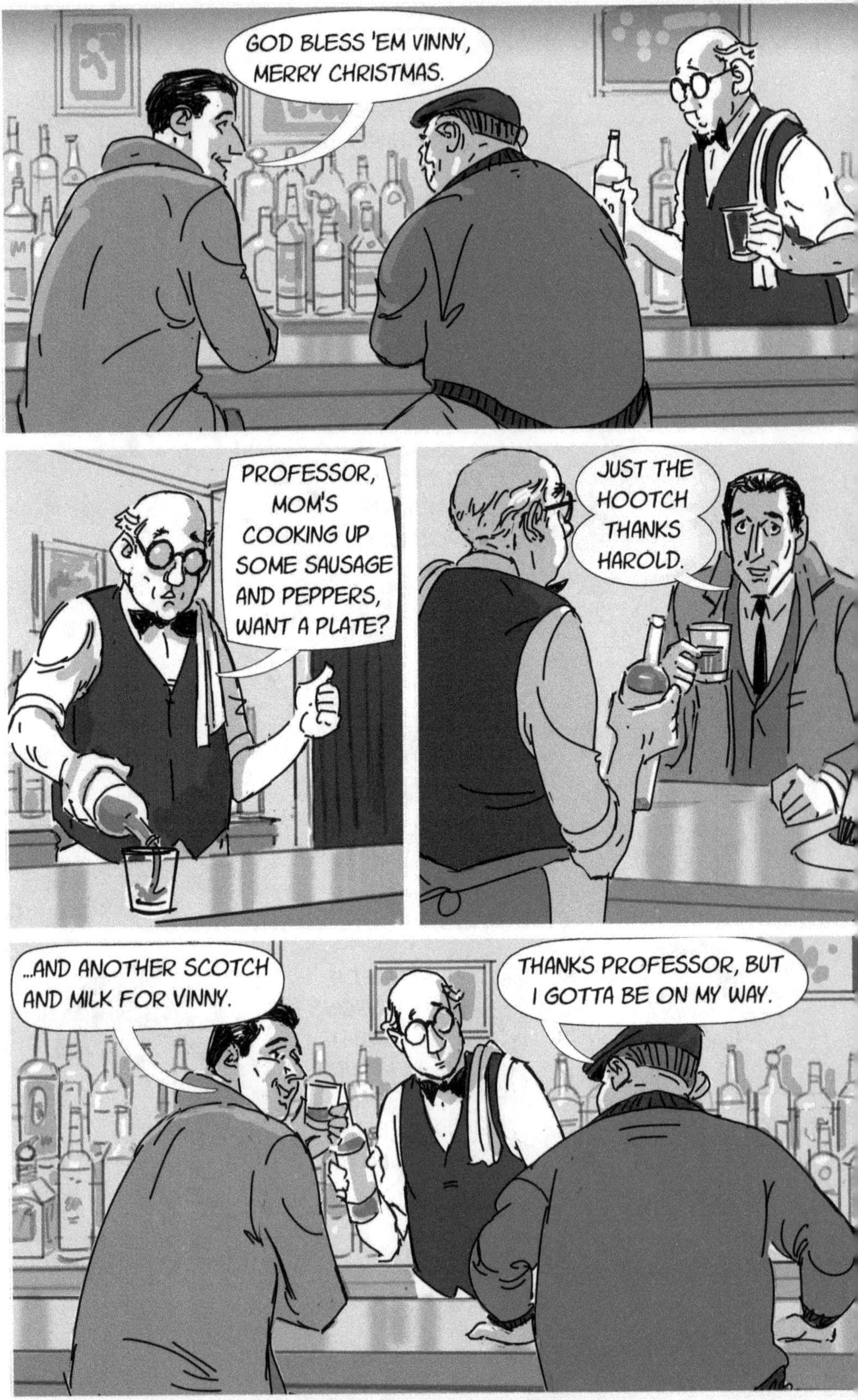
GOD BLESS 'EM VINNY, MERRY CHRISTMAS.
PROFESSOR, MOM'S COOKING UP SOME SAUSAGE AND PEPPERS, WANT A PLATE?
JUST THE HOOTCH THANKS HAROLD.
...AND ANOTHER SCOTCH AND MILK FOR VINNY.
THANKS PROFESSOR, BUT I GOTTA BE ON MY WAY.

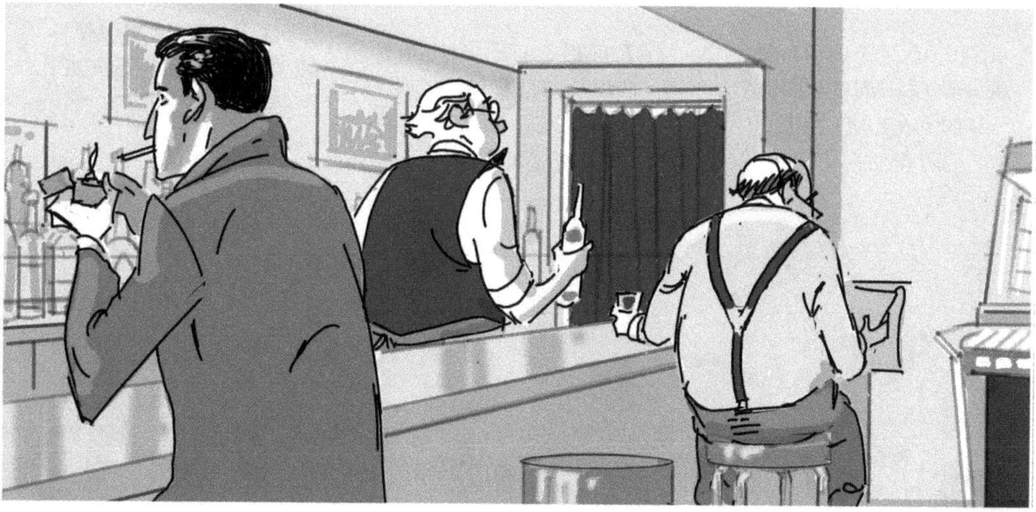

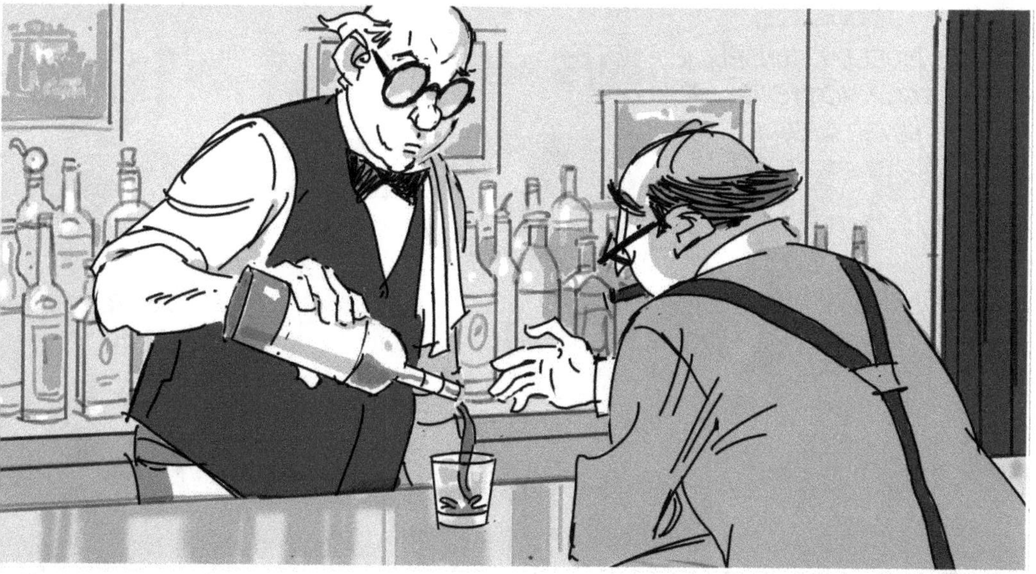

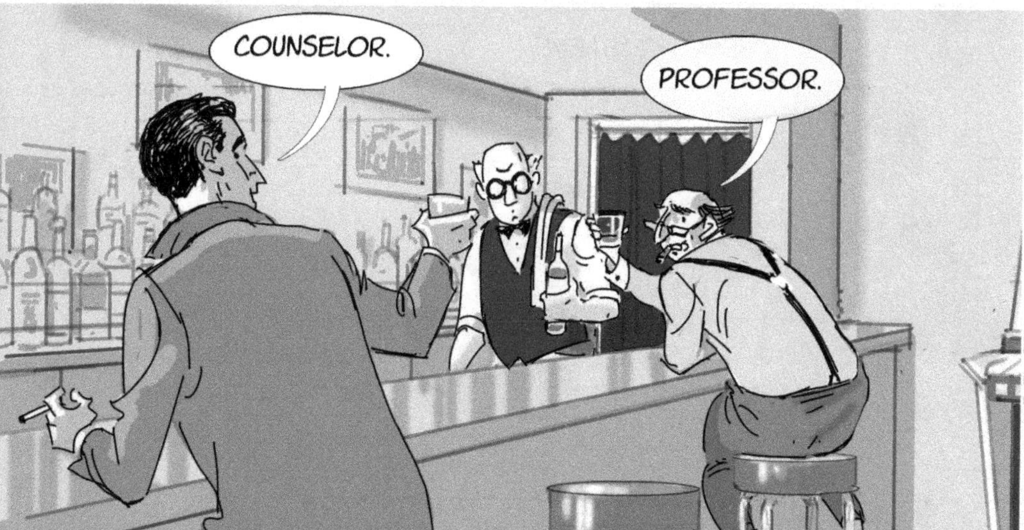
COUNSELOR.
PROFESSOR.

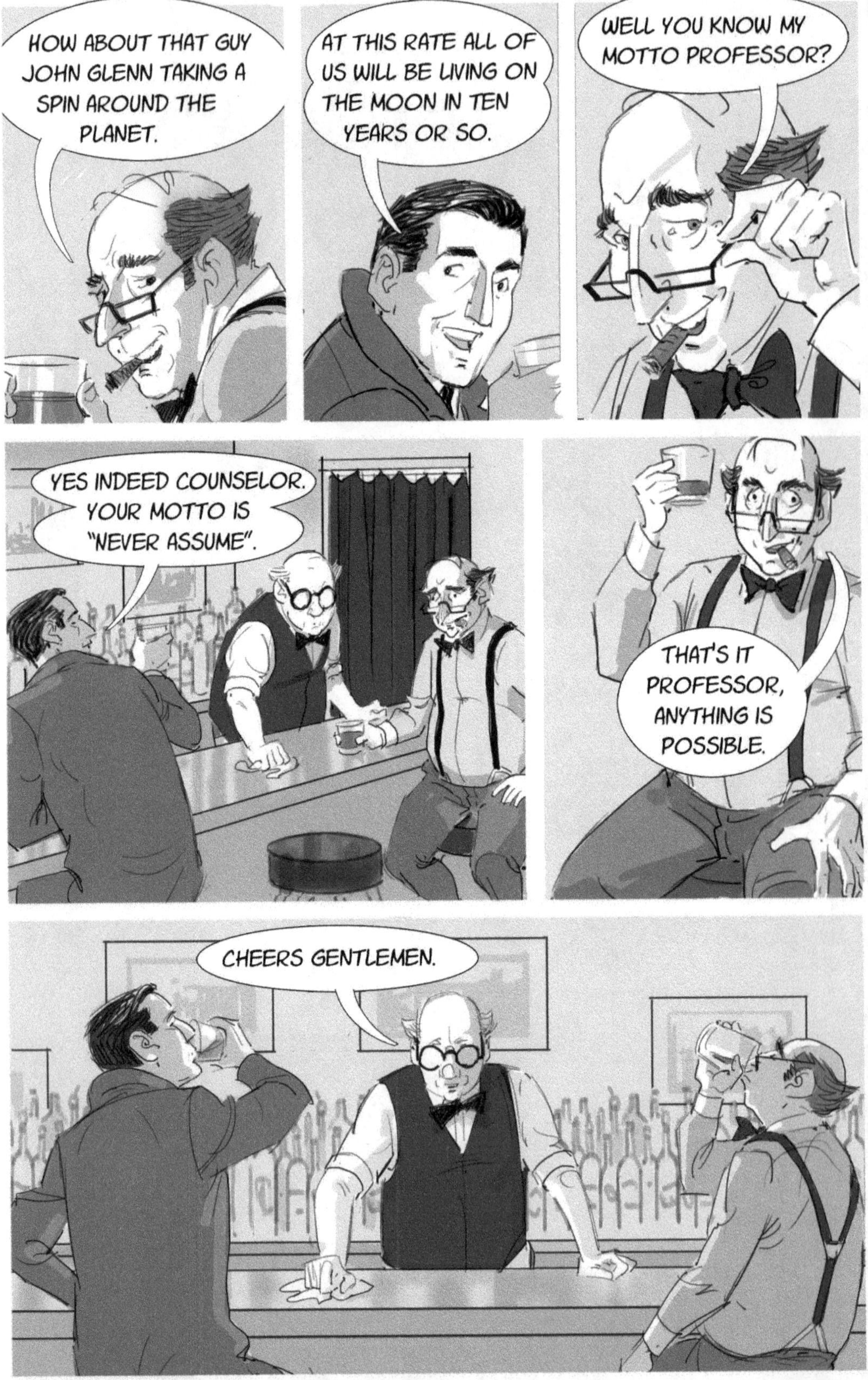
HOW ABOUT THAT GUY JOHN GLENN TAKING A SPIN AROUND THE PLANET.
AT THIS RATE ALL OF US WILL BE LIVING ON THE MOON IN TEN YEARS OR SO.
WELL YOU KNOW MY MOTTO PROFESSOR?
YES INDEED COUNSELOR. YOUR MOTTO IS "NEVER ASSUME".
THAT'S IT PROFESSOR, ANYTHING IS POSSIBLE.
CHEERS GENTLEMEN.

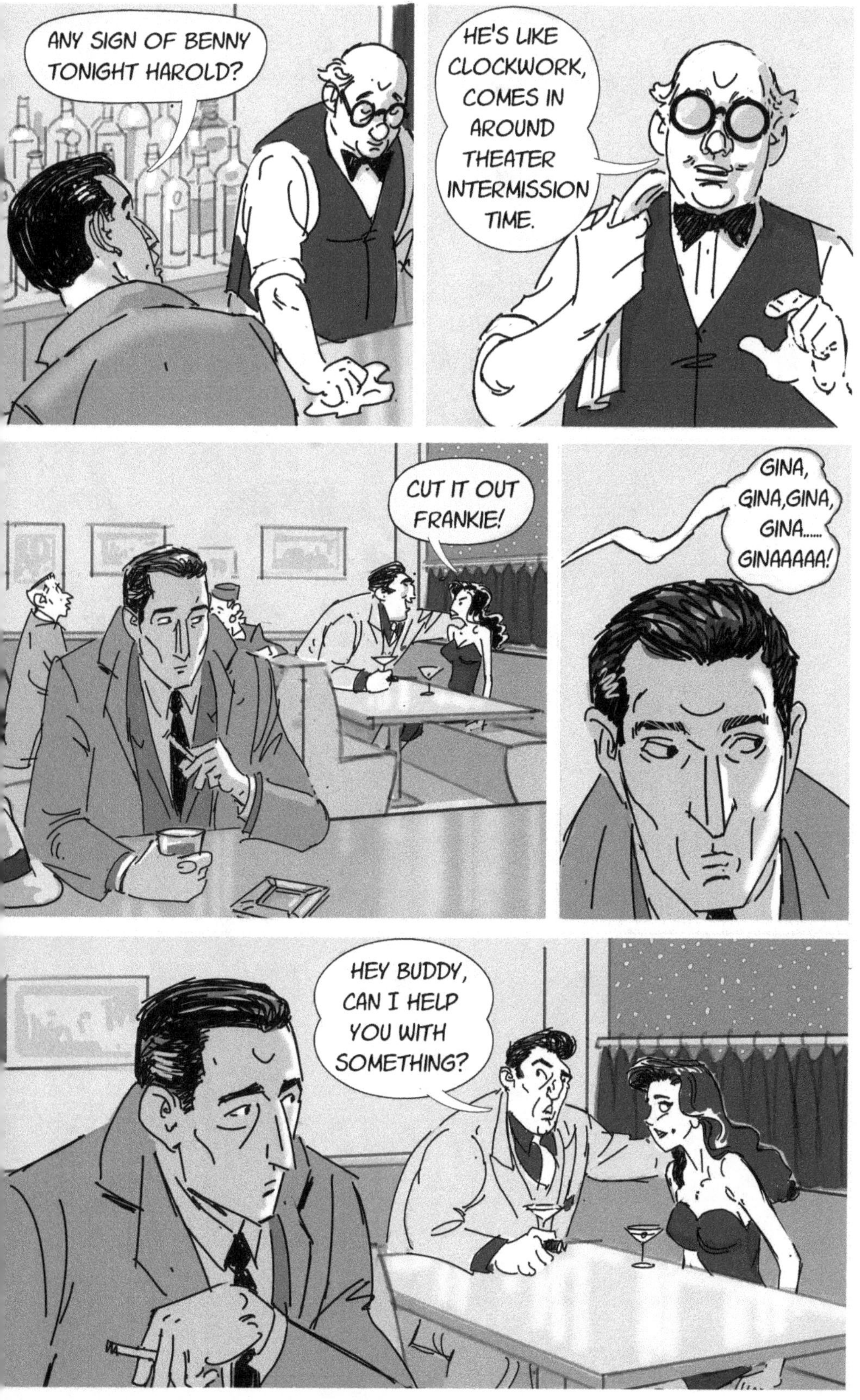
ANY SIGN OF BENNY TONIGHT HAROLD?
HE'S LIKE CLOCKWORK, COMES IN AROUND THEATER INTERMISSION TIME.
CUT IT OUT FRANKIE!
GINA, GINA,GINA, GINA...... GINAAAAAA!
HEY BUDDY, CAN I HELP YOU WITH SOMETHING?

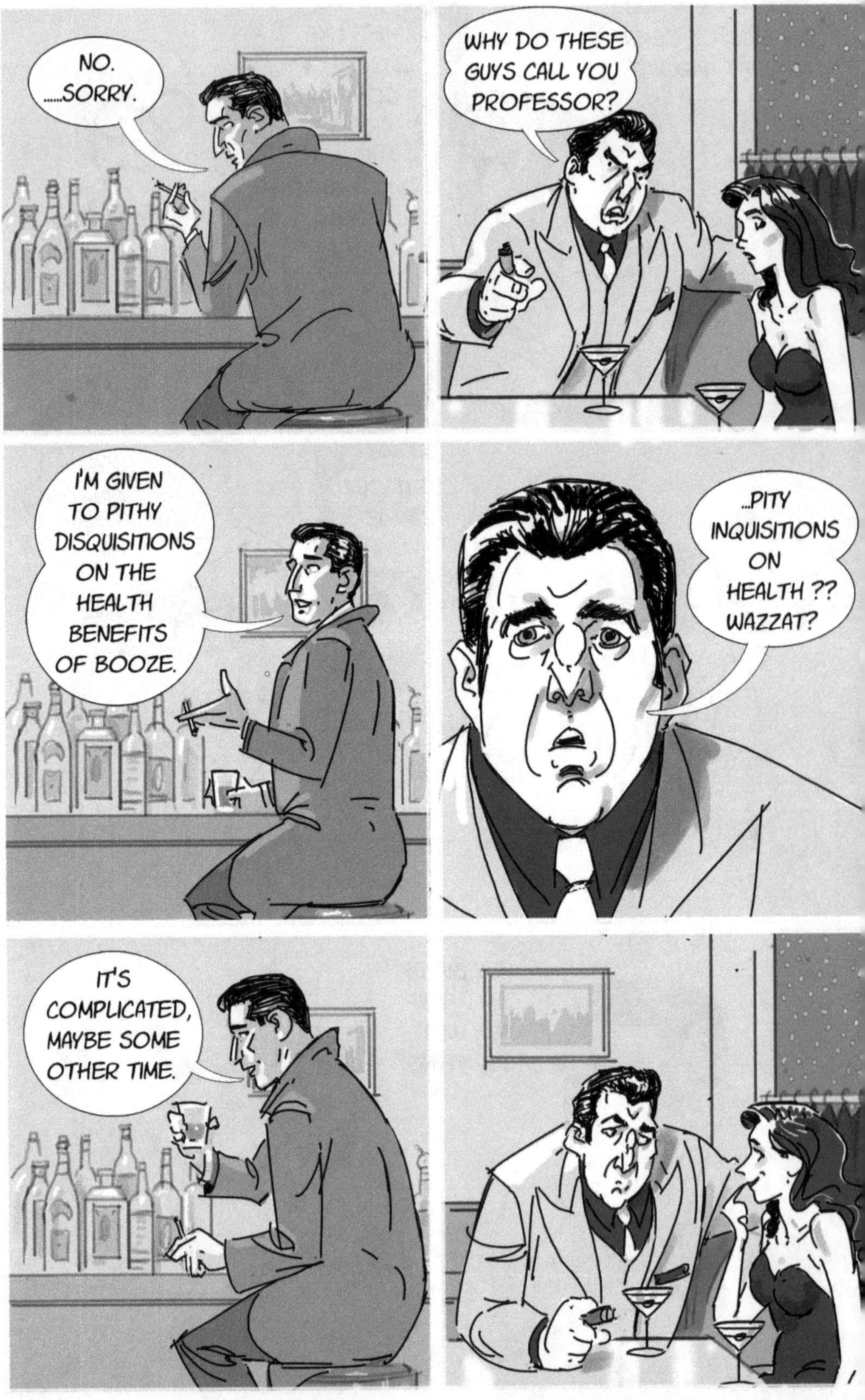
NO. .....SORRY.
WHY DO THESE GUYS CALL YOU PROFESSOR?
I'M GIVEN TO PITHY DISQUISITIONS ON THE HEALTH BENEFITS OF BOOZE.
...PITY INQUISITIONS ON HEALTH ?? WAZZAT?
IT'S COMPLICATED, MAYBE SOME OTHER TIME.

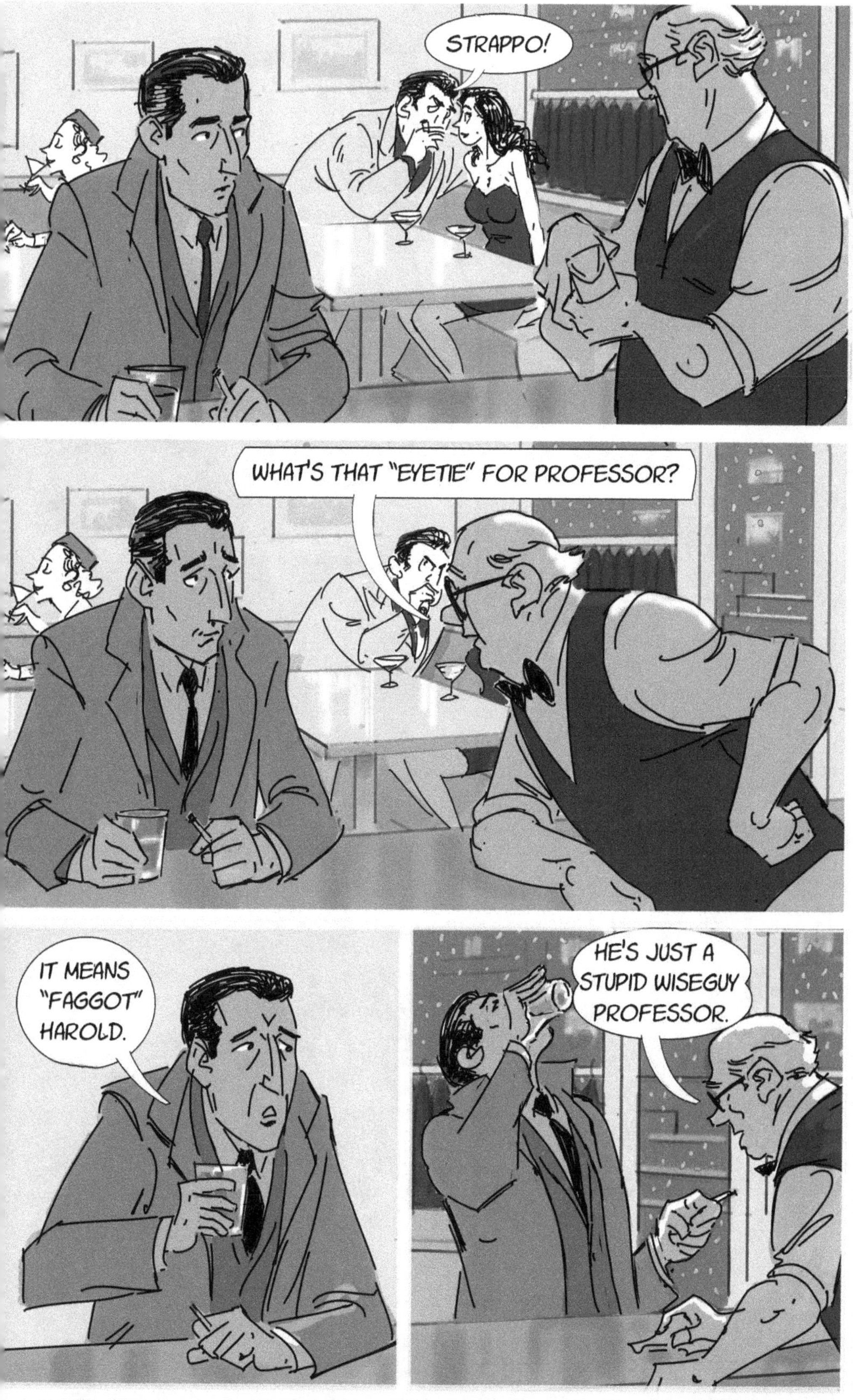
STRAPPO!
WHAT'S THAT "EYETIE" FOR PROFESSOR?
IT MEANS "FAGGOT" HAROLD.
HE'S JUST A STUPID WISEGUY PROFESSOR.

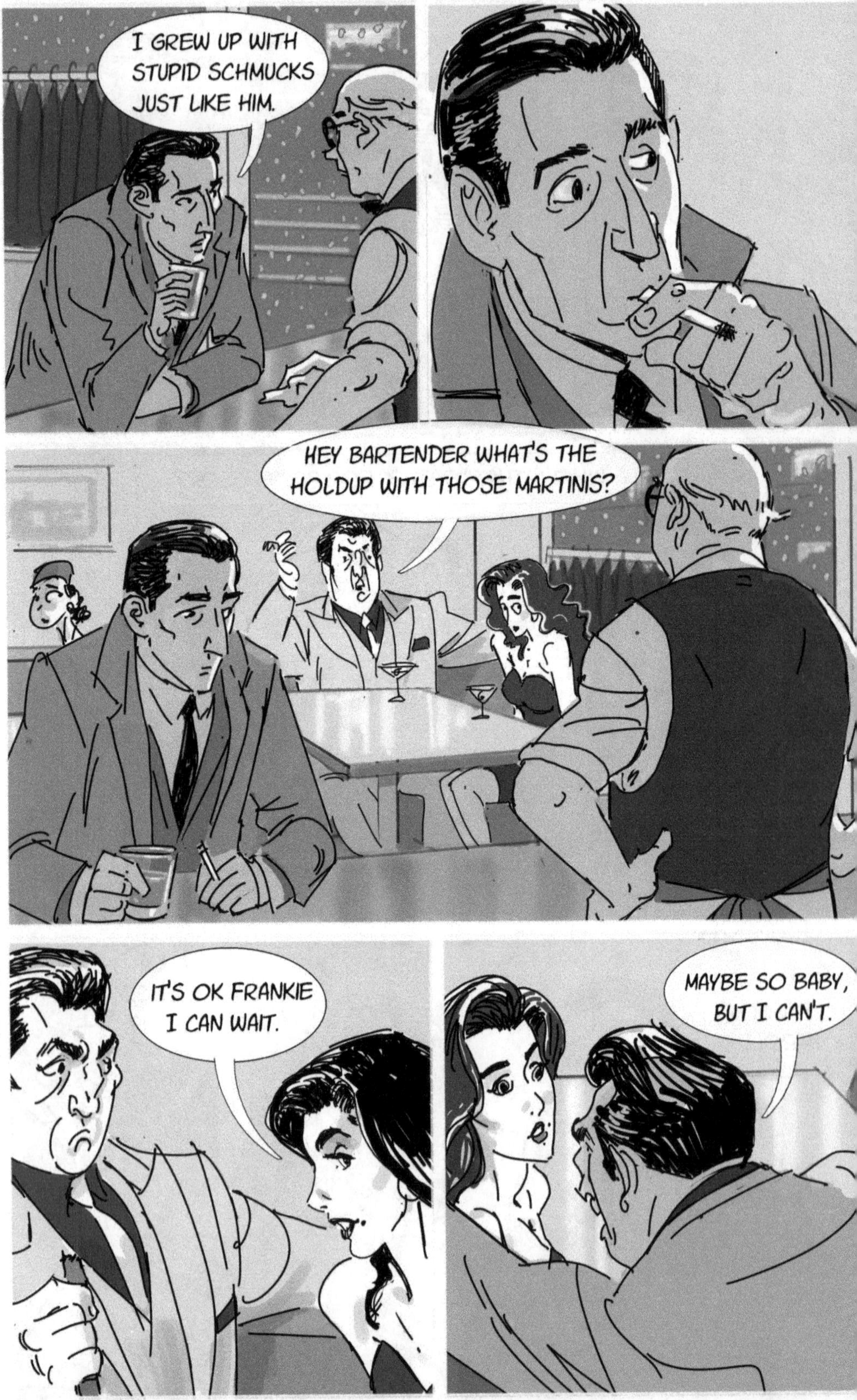
I GREW UP WITH STUPID SCHMUCKS JUST LIKE HIM.
HEY BARTENDER WHAT'S THE HOLDUP WITH THOSE MARTINIS?
IT'S OK FRANKIE I CAN WAIT.
MAYBE SO BABY, BUT I CAN'T.

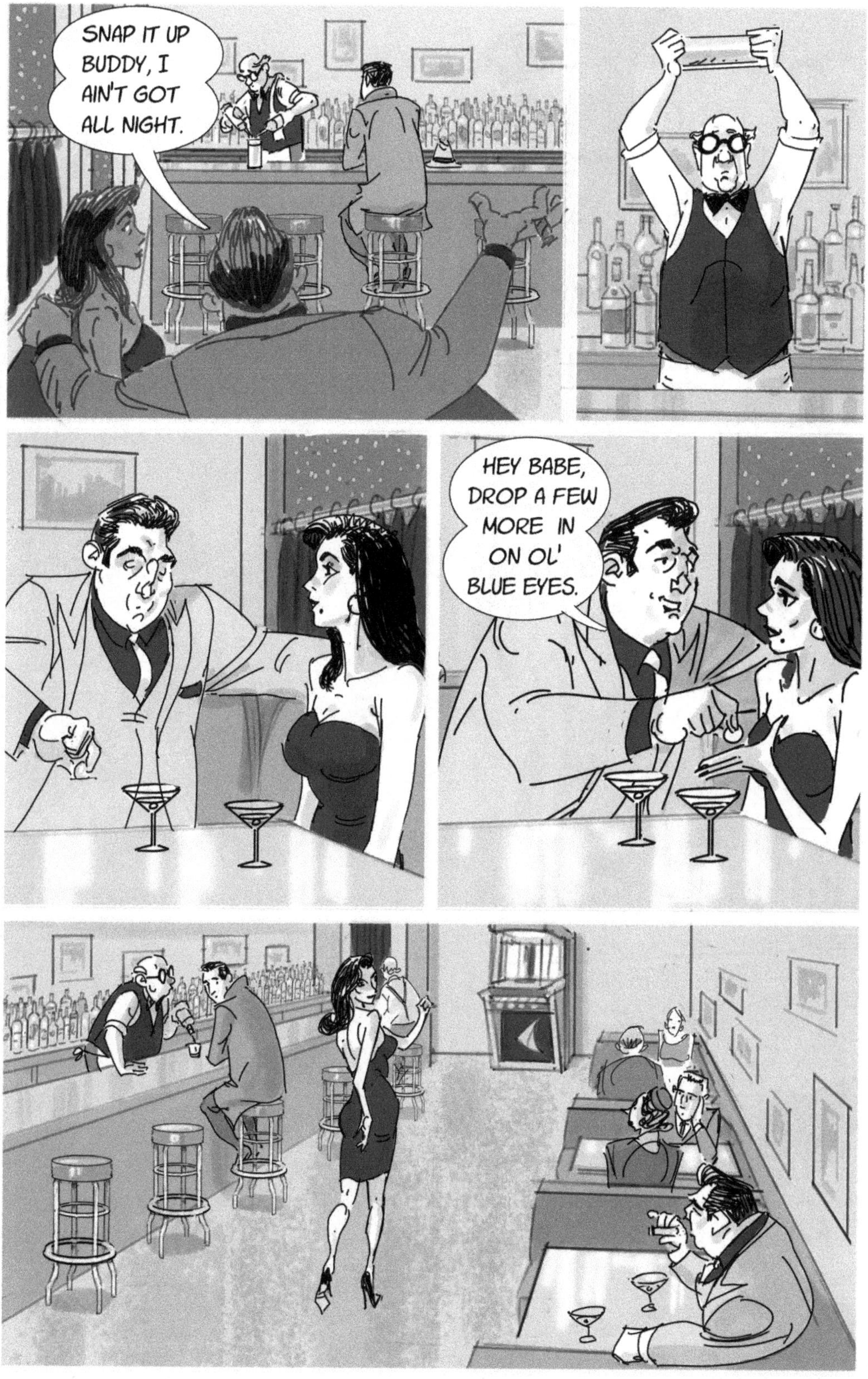
SNAP IT UP BUDDY, I AIN'T GOT ALL NIGHT.
HEY BABE, DROP A FEW MORE IN ON OL' BLUE EYES.

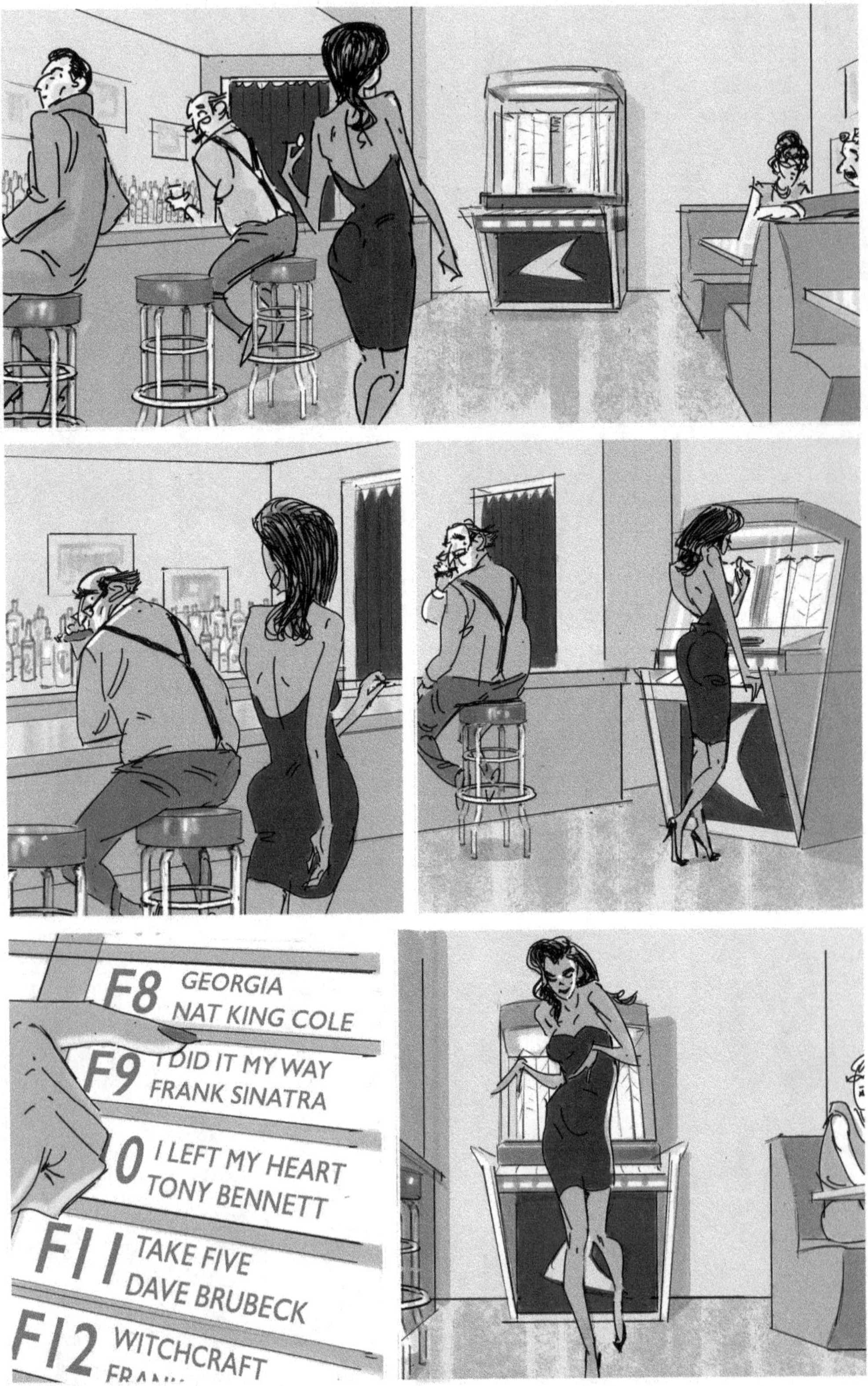
F8 GEORGIA
NAT KING COLE
F9 I DID IT MY WAY
FRANK SINATRA
I LEFT MY HEART
TONY BENNETT
F11 TAKE FIVE
DAVE BRUBECK
F12 WITCHCRAFT

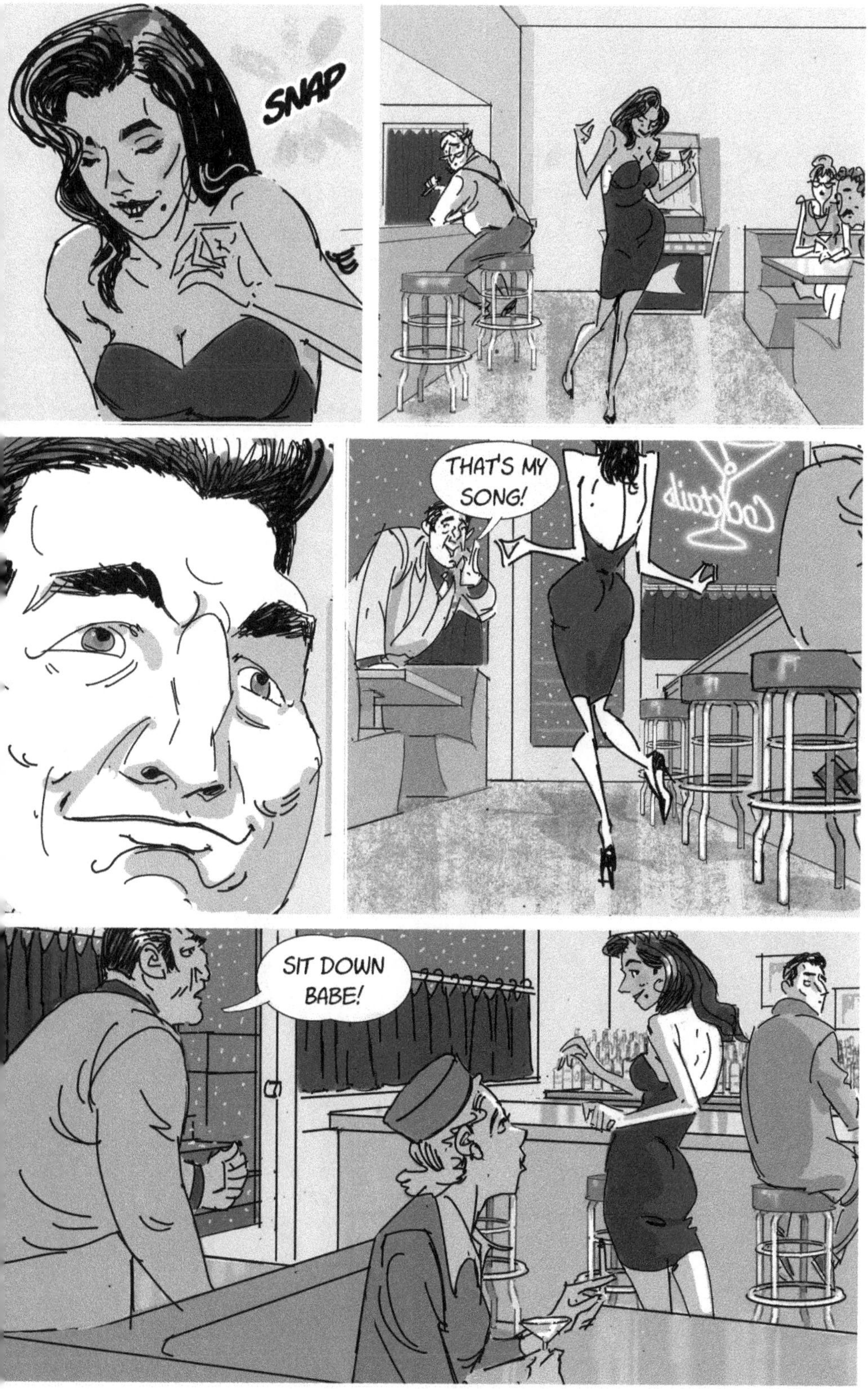
SNAP
THAT'S MY SONG!
Cocktails
SIT DOWN BABE!

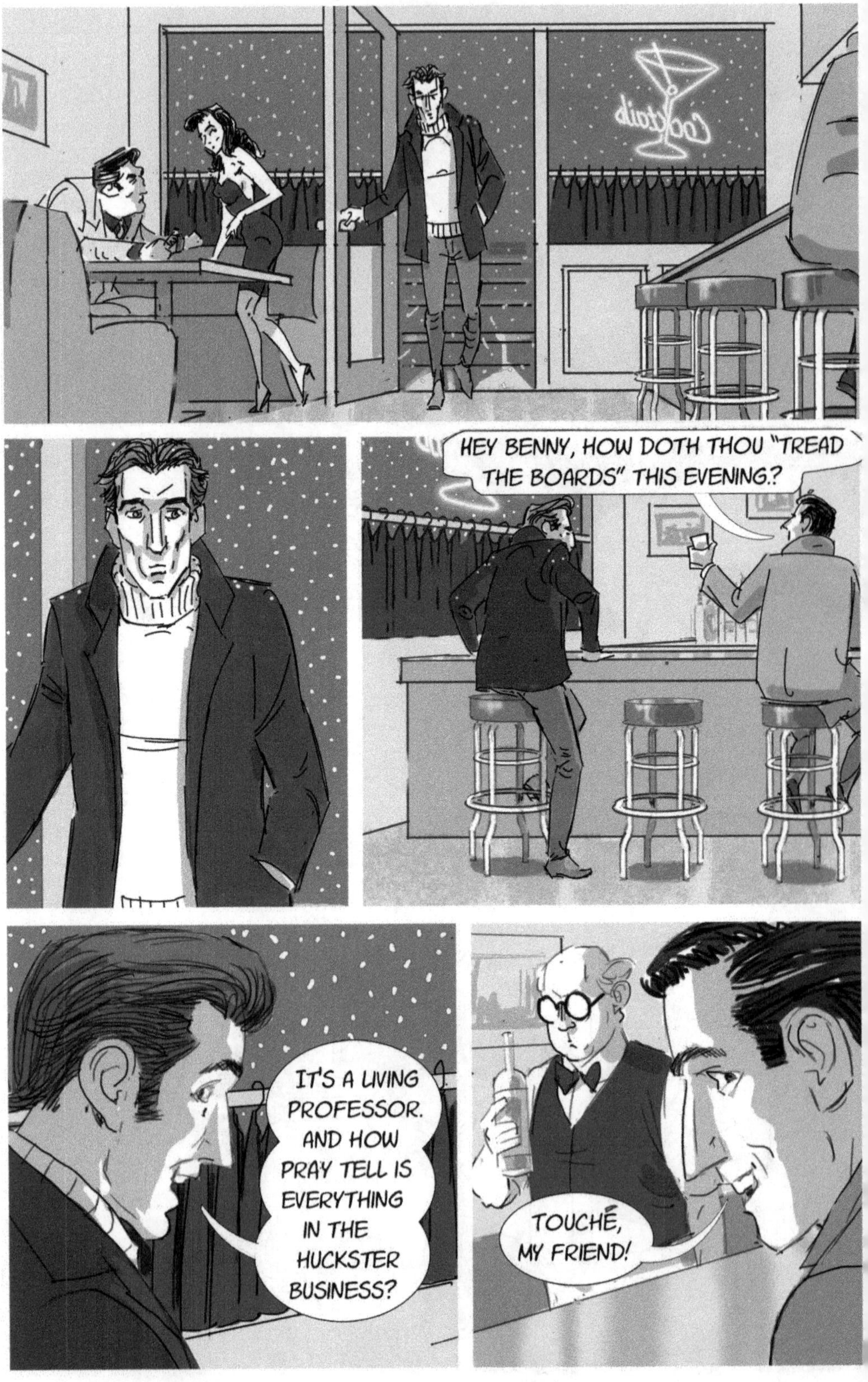
Cocktails
HEY BENNY, HOW DOTH THOU "TREAD THE BOARDS" THIS EVENING.?
IT'S A LIVING PROFESSOR. AND HOW PRAY TELL IS EVERYTHING IN THE HUCKSTER BUSINESS?
TOUCHÉ, MY FRIEND!

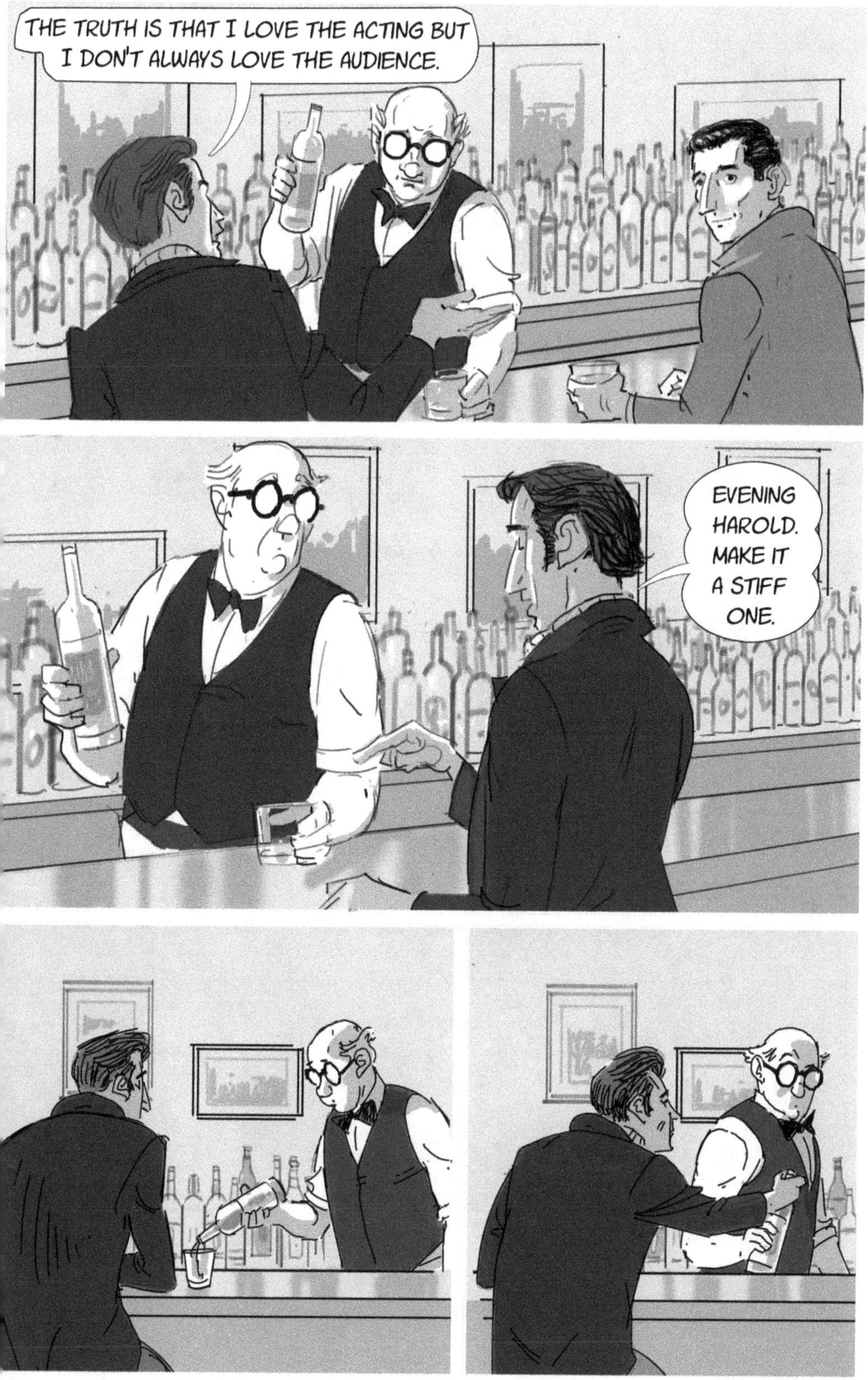
THE TRUTH IS THAT I LOVE THE ACTING BUT I DON'T ALWAYS LOVE THE AUDIENCE.
EVENING HAROLD. MAKE IT A STIFF ONE.

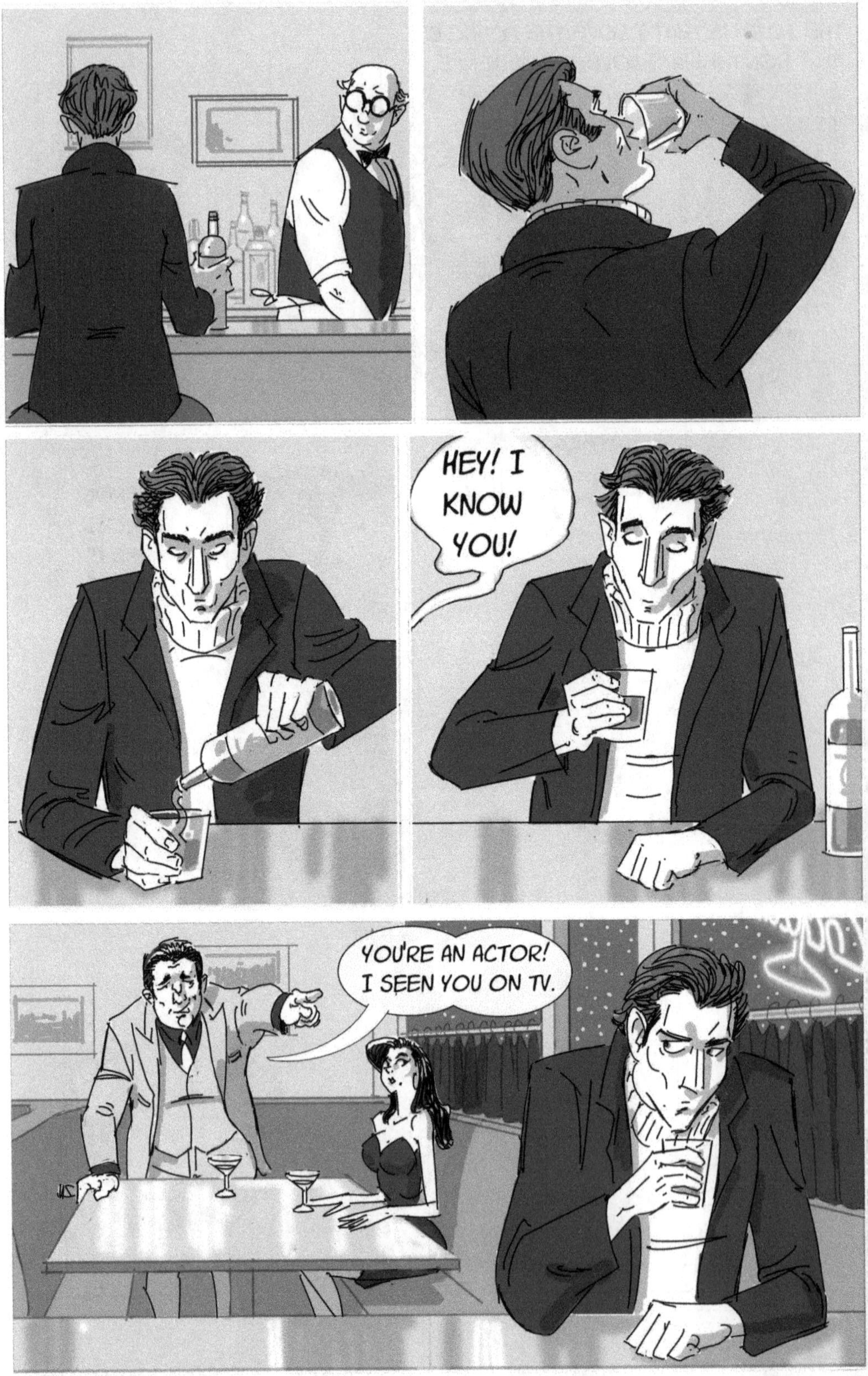
HEY! I KNOW YOU!
YOU'RE AN ACTOR! I SEEN YOU ON TV.

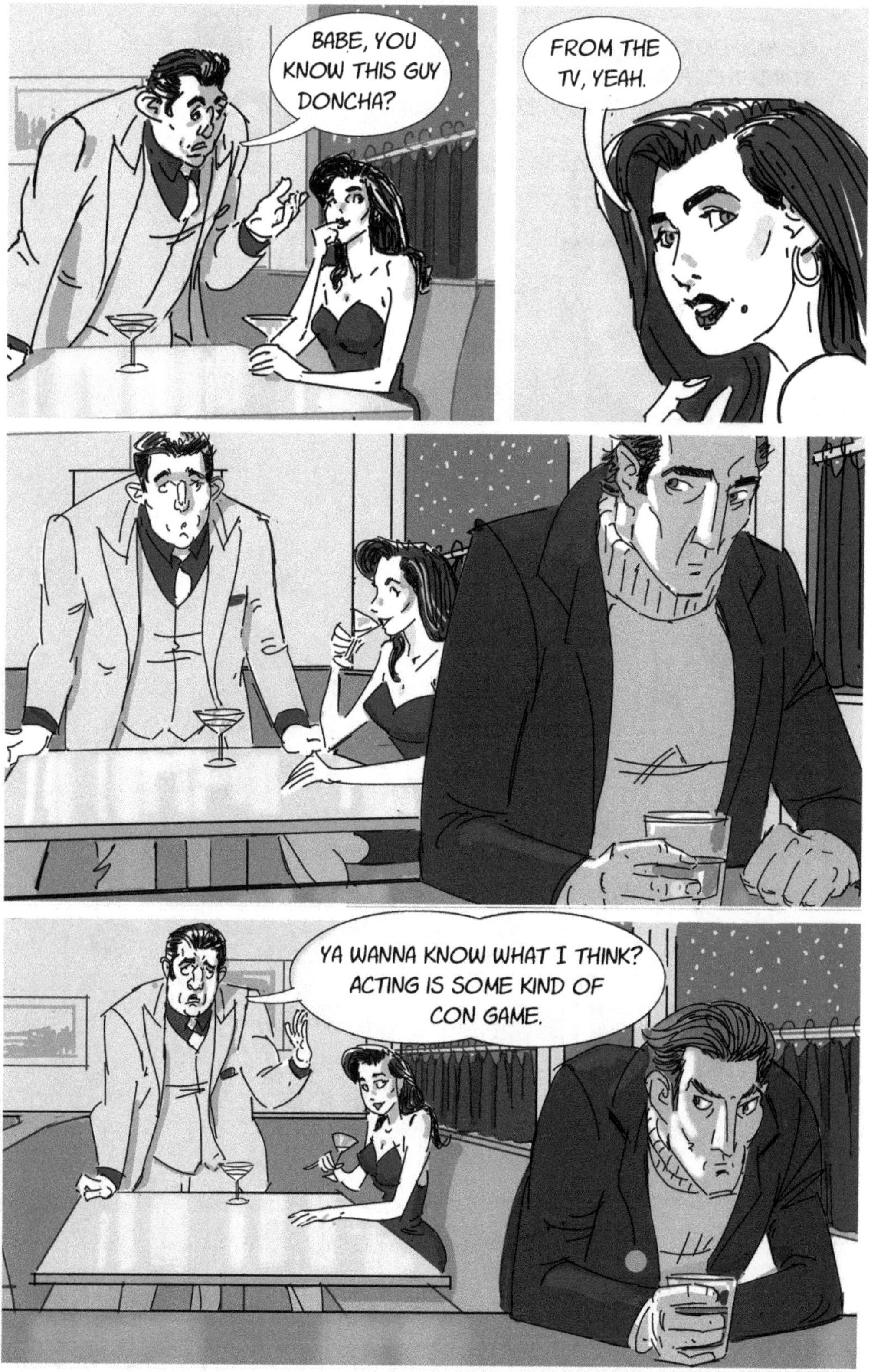
BABE, YOU KNOW THIS GUY DONCHA?
FROM THE TV, YEAH.
YA WANNA KNOW WHAT I THINK? ACTING IS SOME KIND OF CON GAME.

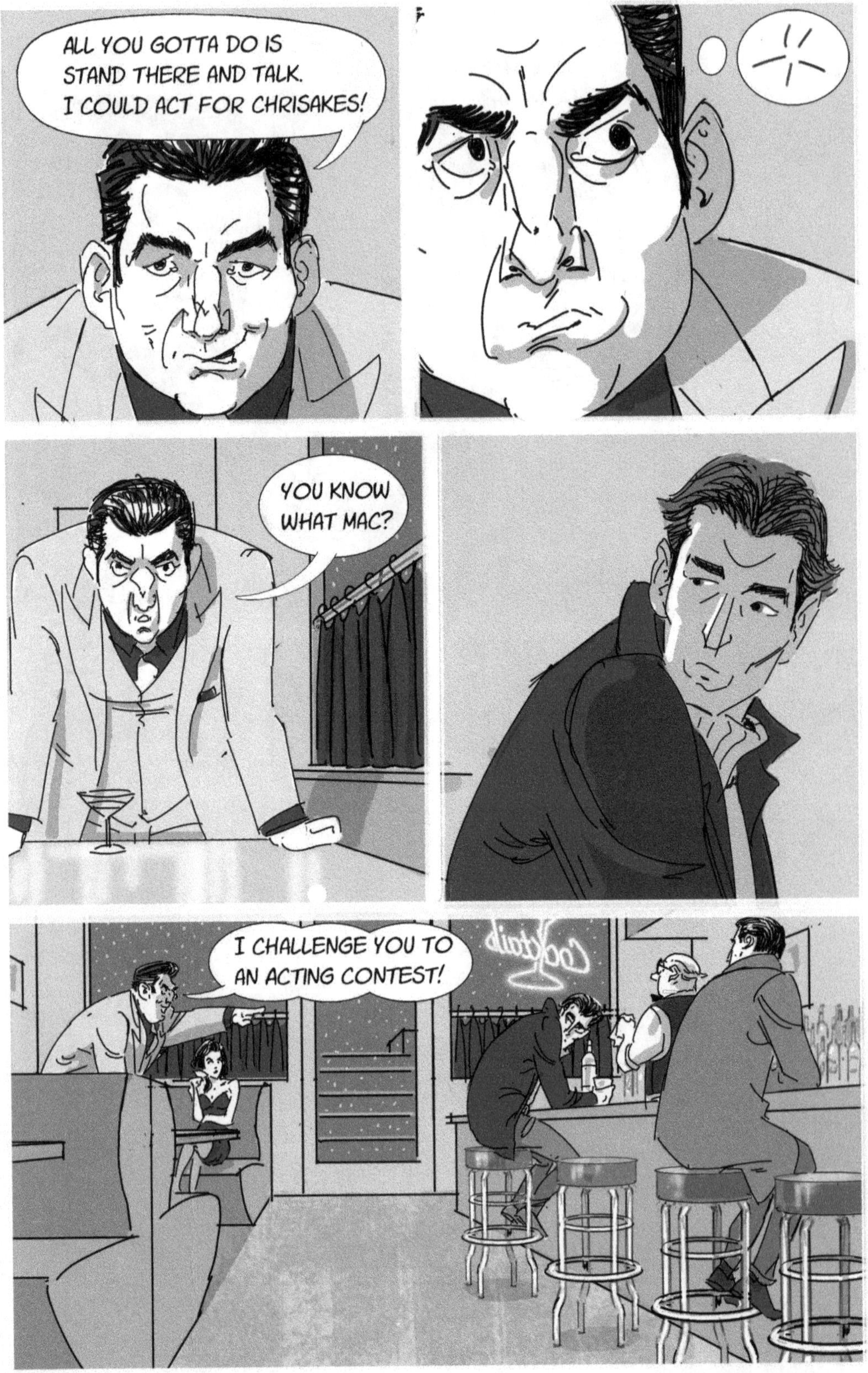
ALL YOU GOTTA DO IS STAND THERE AND TALK. I COULD ACT FOR CHRISAKES!
YOU KNOW WHAT MAC?
I CHALLENGE YOU TO AN ACTING CONTEST!

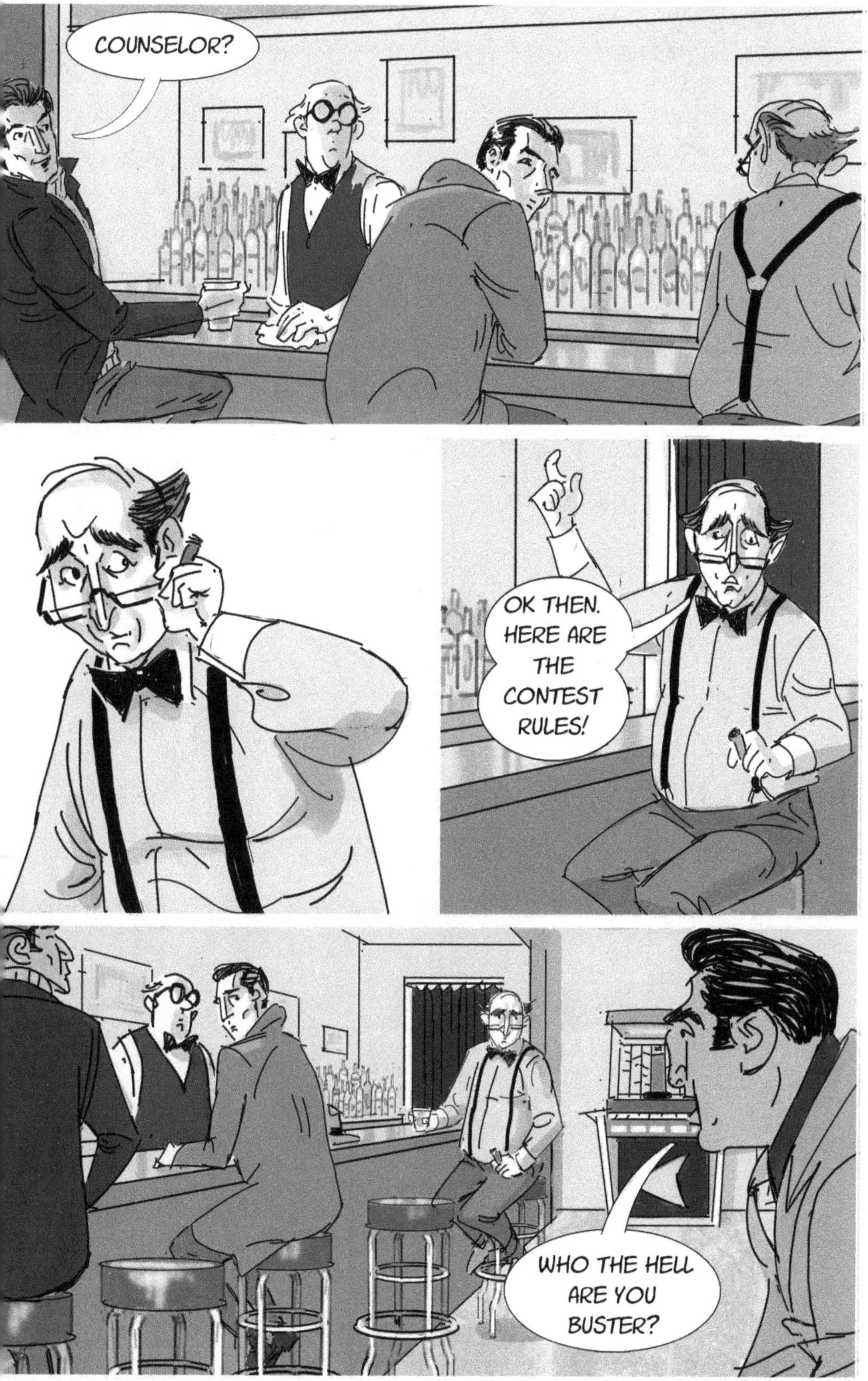
COUNSELOR?
OK THEN. HERE ARE THE CONTEST RULES!
WHO THE HELL ARE YOU BUSTER?

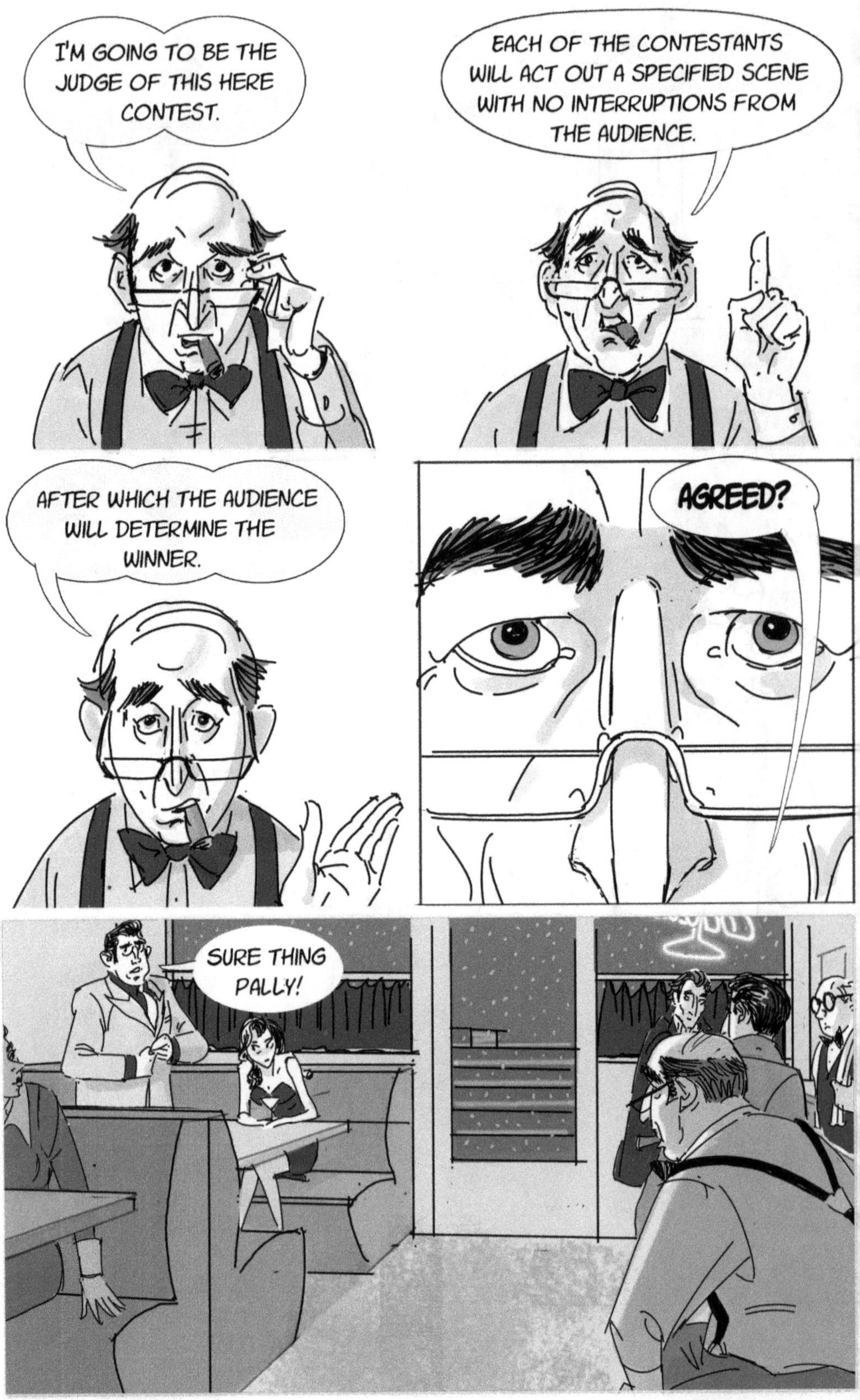

I'M GOING TO BE THE JUDGE OF THIS HERE CONTEST.
EACH OF THE CONTESTANTS WILL ACT OUT A SPECIFIED SCENE WITH NO INTERRUPTIONS FROM THE AUDIENCE.
AFTER WHICH THE AUDIENCE WILL DETERMINE THE WINNER.
AGREED?
SURE THING PALLY!

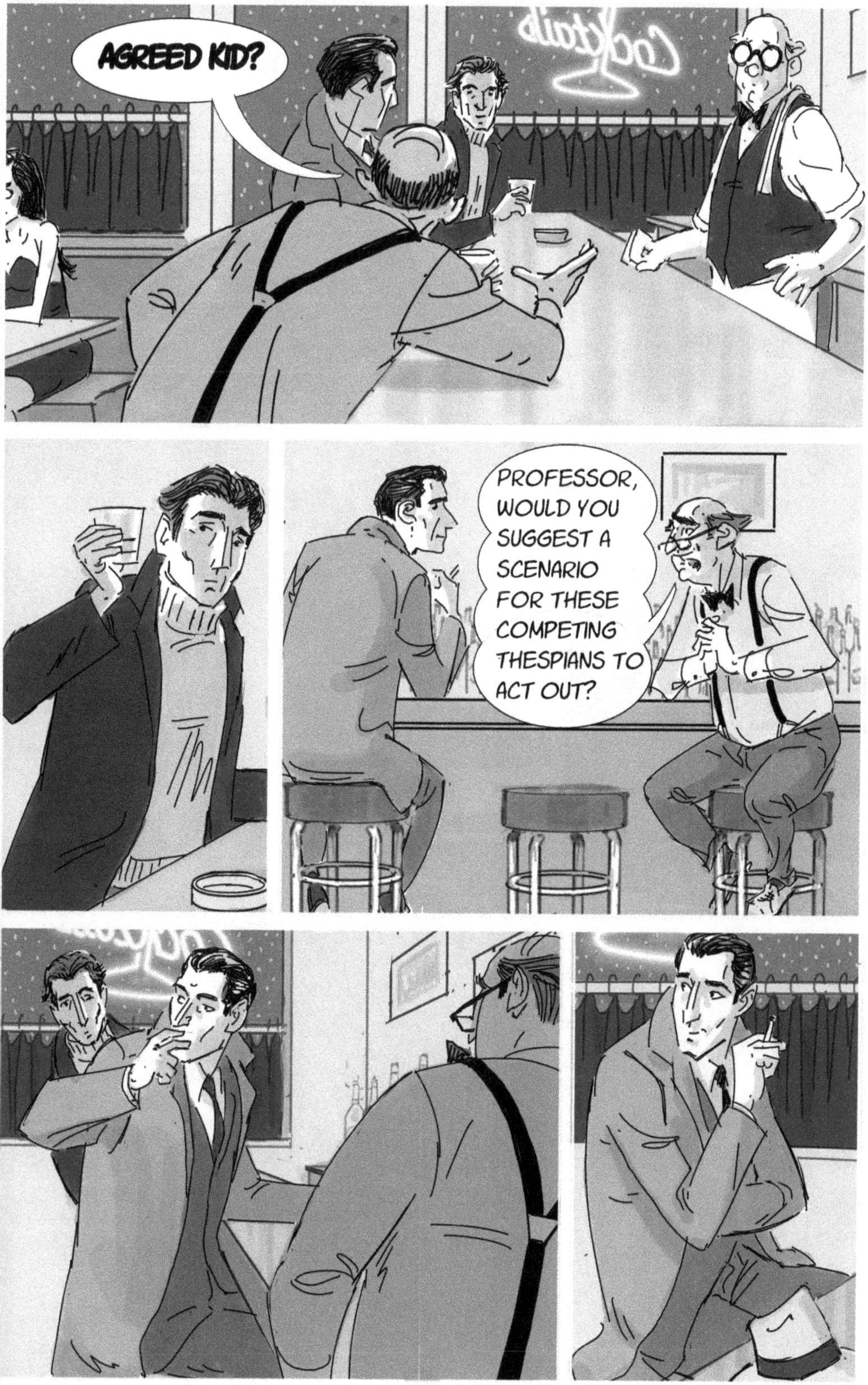
AGREED KID?
PROFESSOR, WOULD YOU SUGGEST A SCENARIO FOR THESE COMPETING THESPIANS TO ACT OUT?

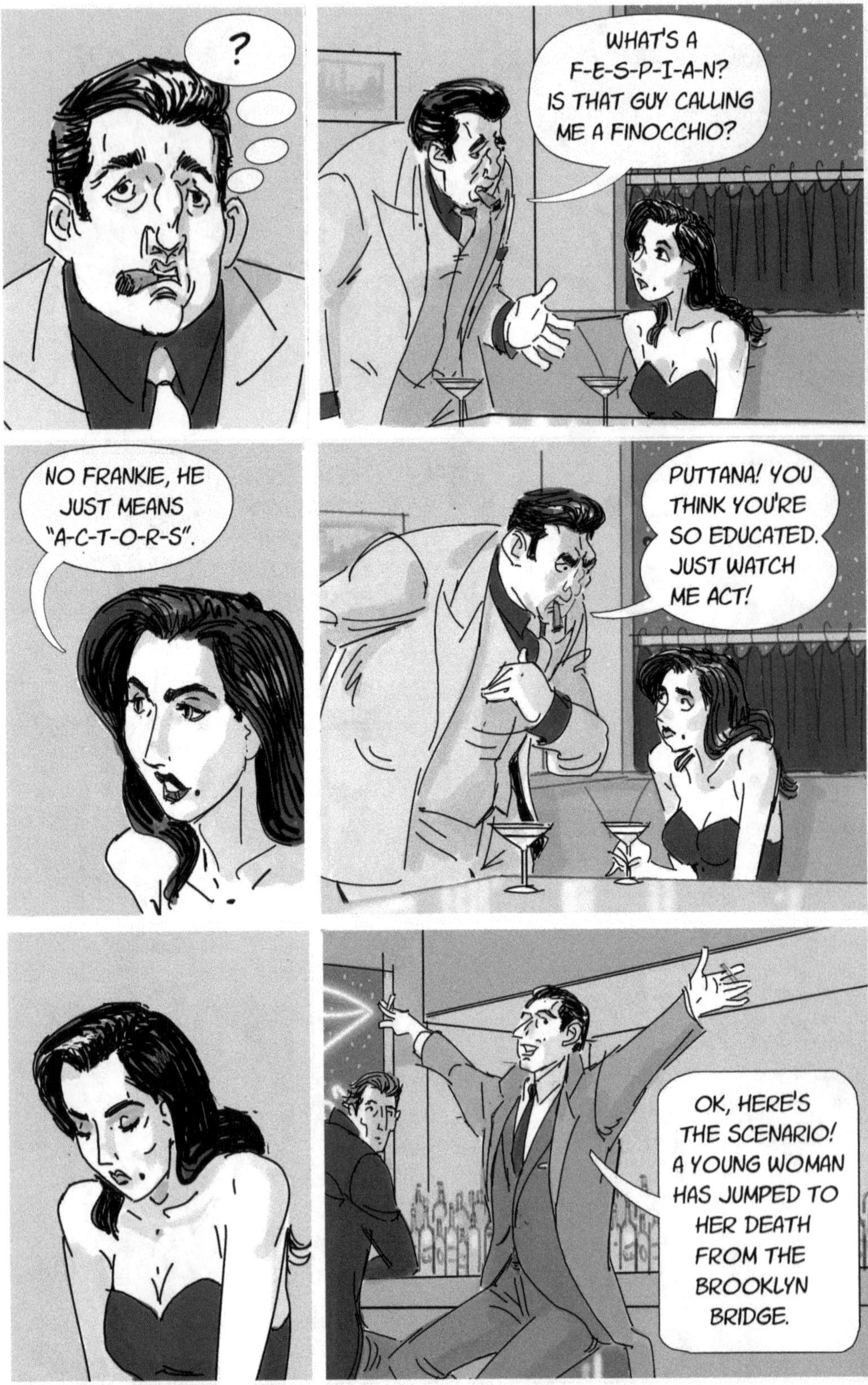
?
WHAT'S A F-E-S-P-I-A-N? IS THAT GUY CALLING ME A FINOCCHIO?
NO FRANKIE, HE JUST MEANS "A-C-T-O-R-S".
PUTTANA! YOU THINK YOU'RE SO EDUCATED. JUST WATCH ME ACT!
OK, HERE'S THE SCENARIO! A YOUNG WOMAN HAS JUMPED TO HER DEATH FROM THE BROOKLYN BRIDGE.

EACH CONTESTANT WILL PLAY THE PART OF THE FATHER AS HE REACTS TO THE NEWS OF HIS DAUGHTER'S SUICIDE.

GREAT!

OK, HEADS THE KID GOES FIRST.

TAILS, THE CHALLENGER GOES FIRST.

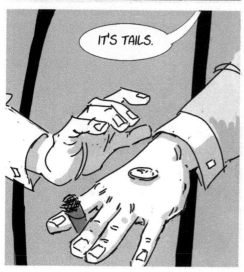

IT'S TAILS.

THE STAGE BELONGS TO THE CHALLENGER.

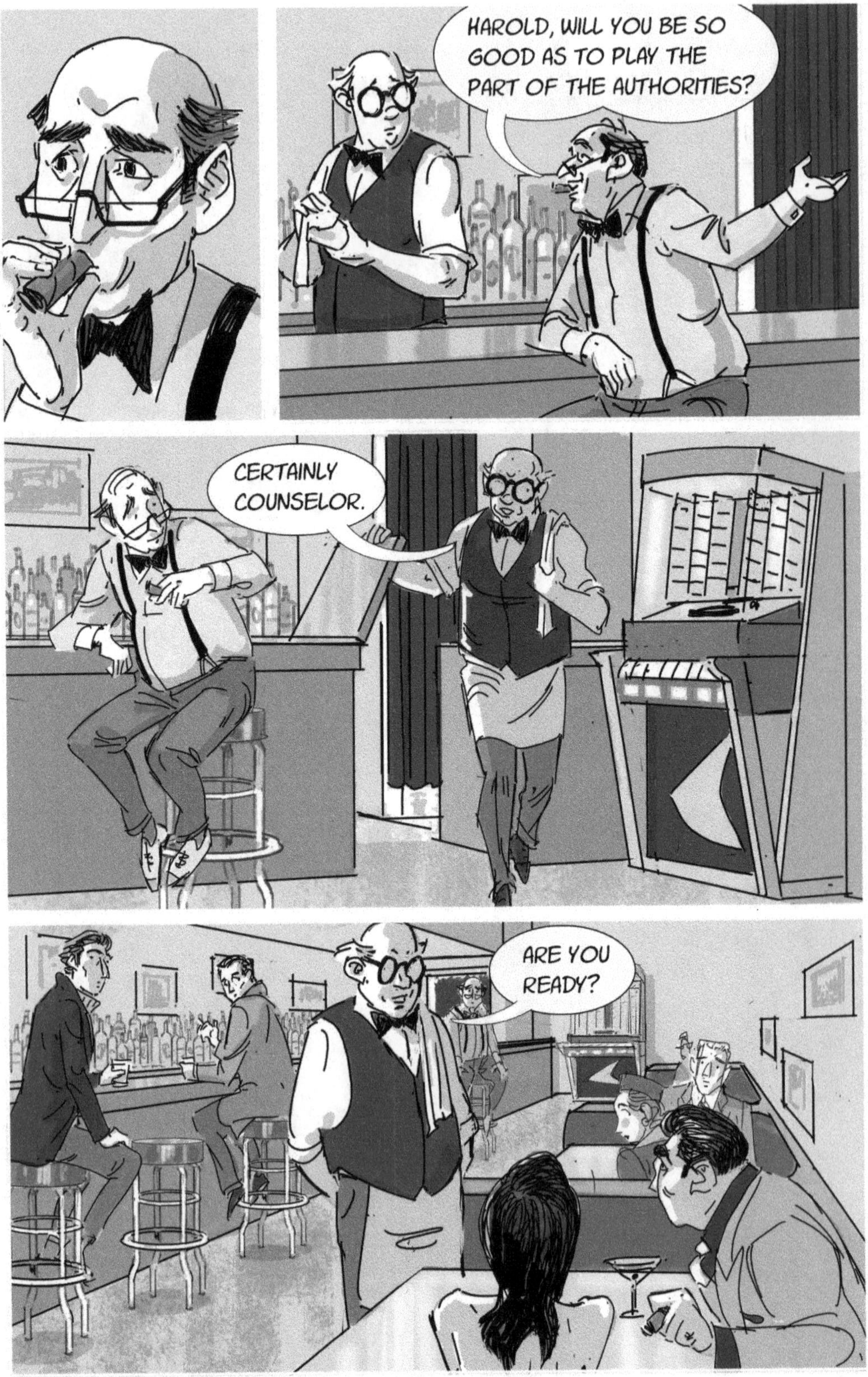
HAROLD, WILL YOU BE SO GOOD AS TO PLAY THE PART OF THE AUTHORITIES?
CERTAINLY COUNSELOR.
ARE YOU READY?

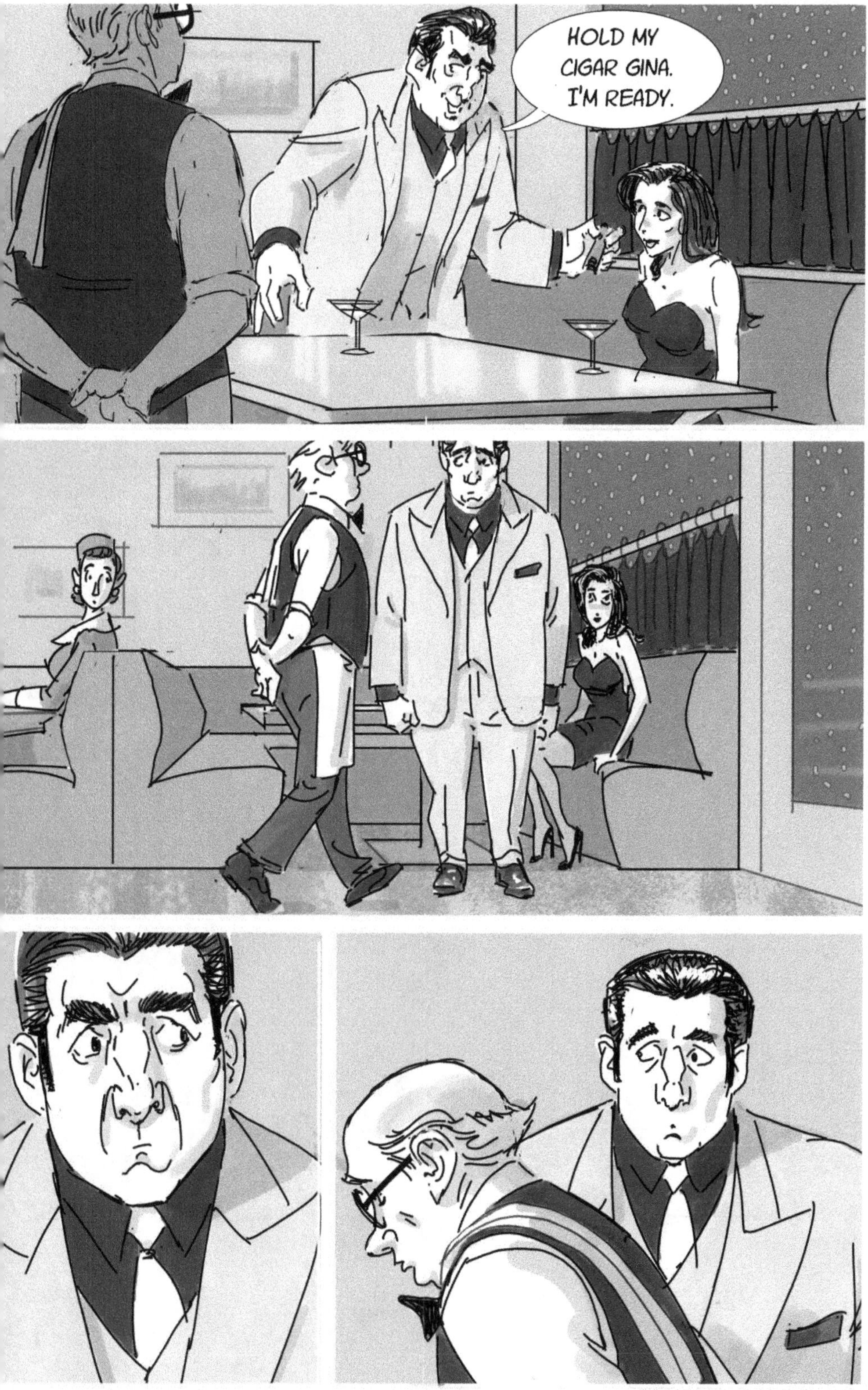
HOLD MY CIGAR GINA. I'M READY.

MR. THROGMORTON, I AM SORRY TO REPORT TO YOU THAT YOUR DAUGHTER JUMPED TO HER DEATH FROM THE BROOKLYN BRIDGE AT 4 O'CLOCK THIS MORNING.

WHAAATTT?

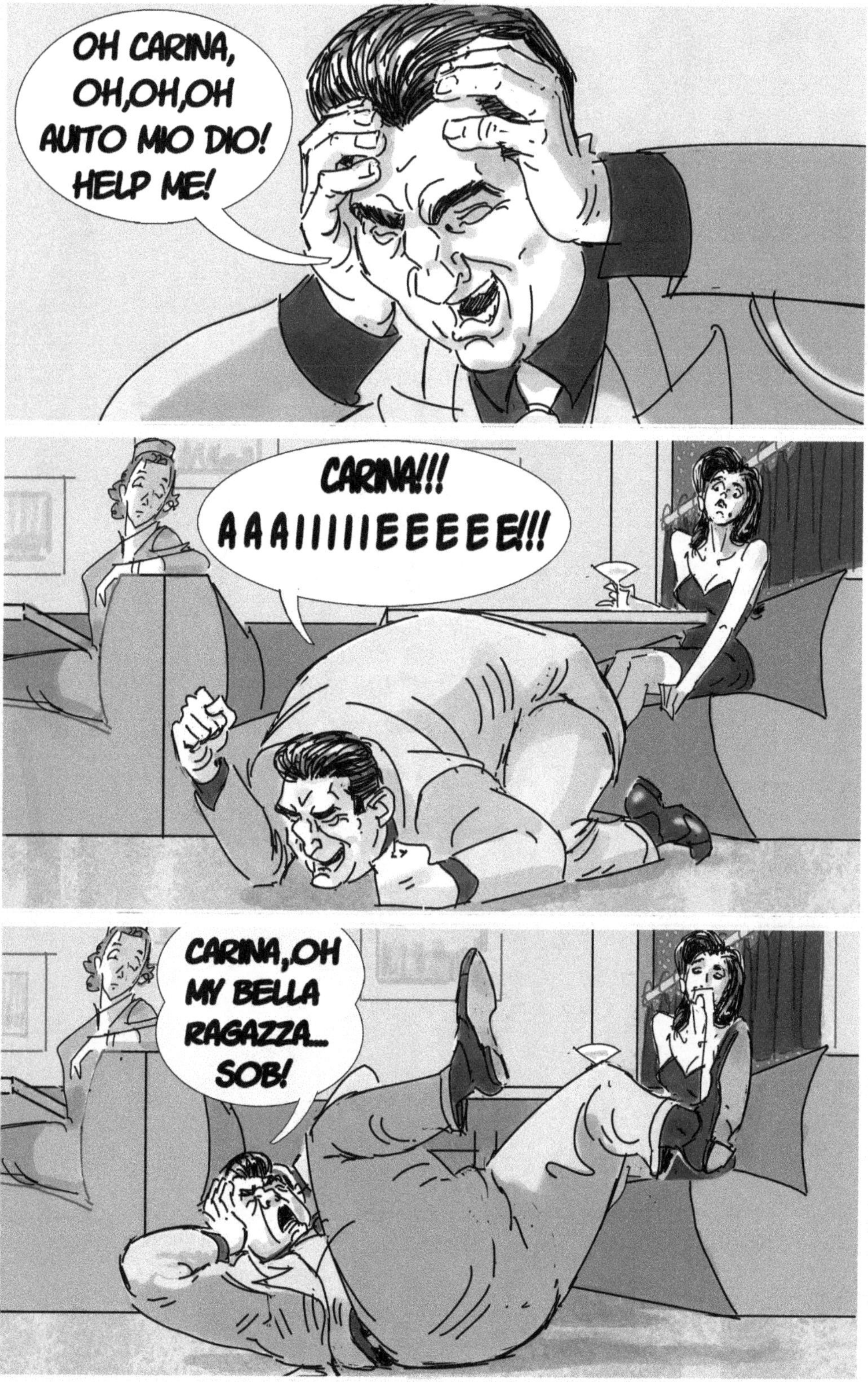
OH CARINA, OH,OH,OH AUITO MIO DIO! HELP ME!
CARINA!!! AAAIIIIIEEEEEE!!!
CARINA, OH MY BELLA RAGAZZA... SOB!

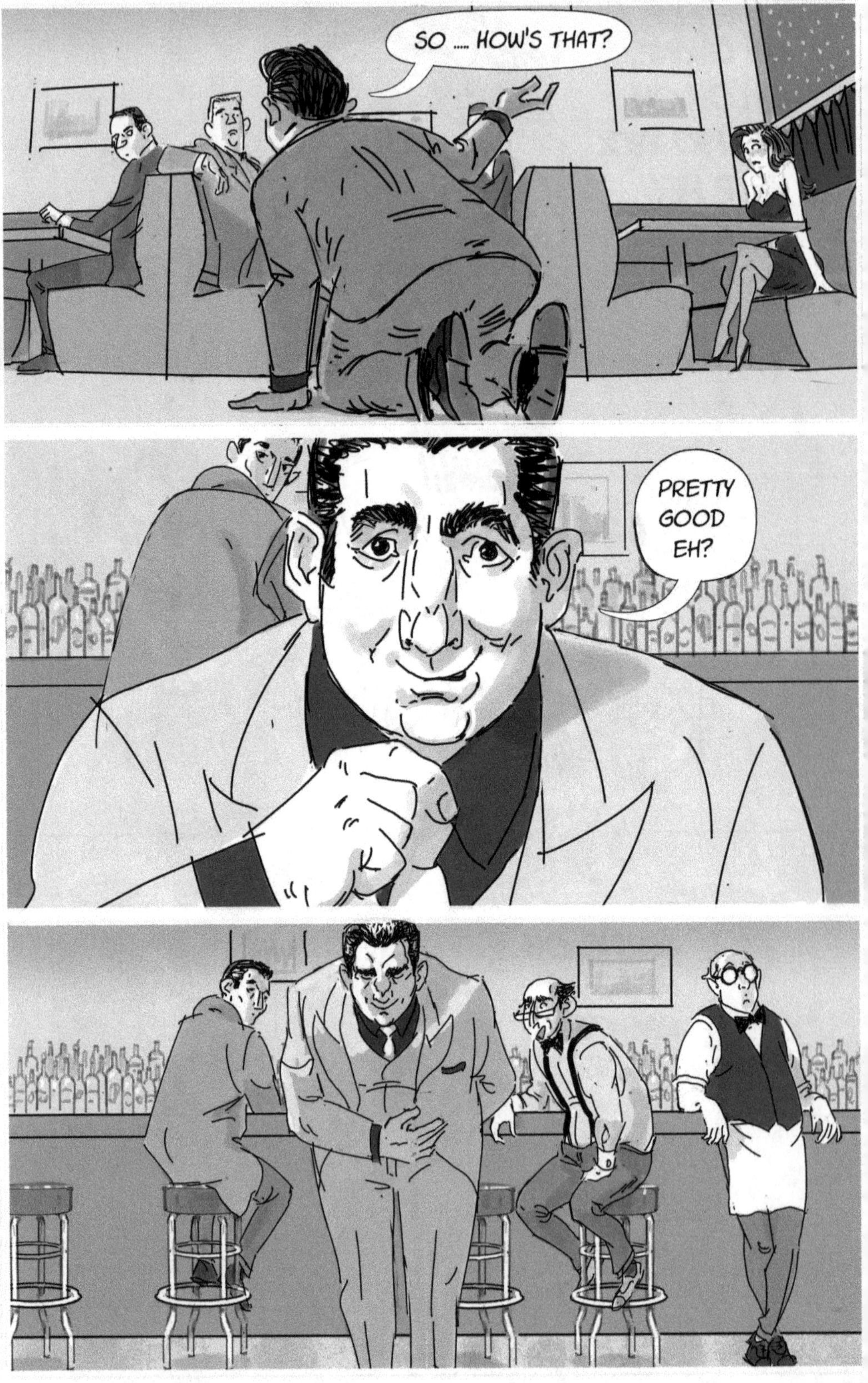
SO .... HOW'S THAT?
PRETTY GOOD EH?

READY KID?

READY HAROLD.

MR. THROGMORTON, I AM SORRY TO REPORT TO YOU THAT YOUR DAUGHTER JUMPED TO HER DEATH FROM THE BROOKLYN BRIDGE AT 4 A.M.

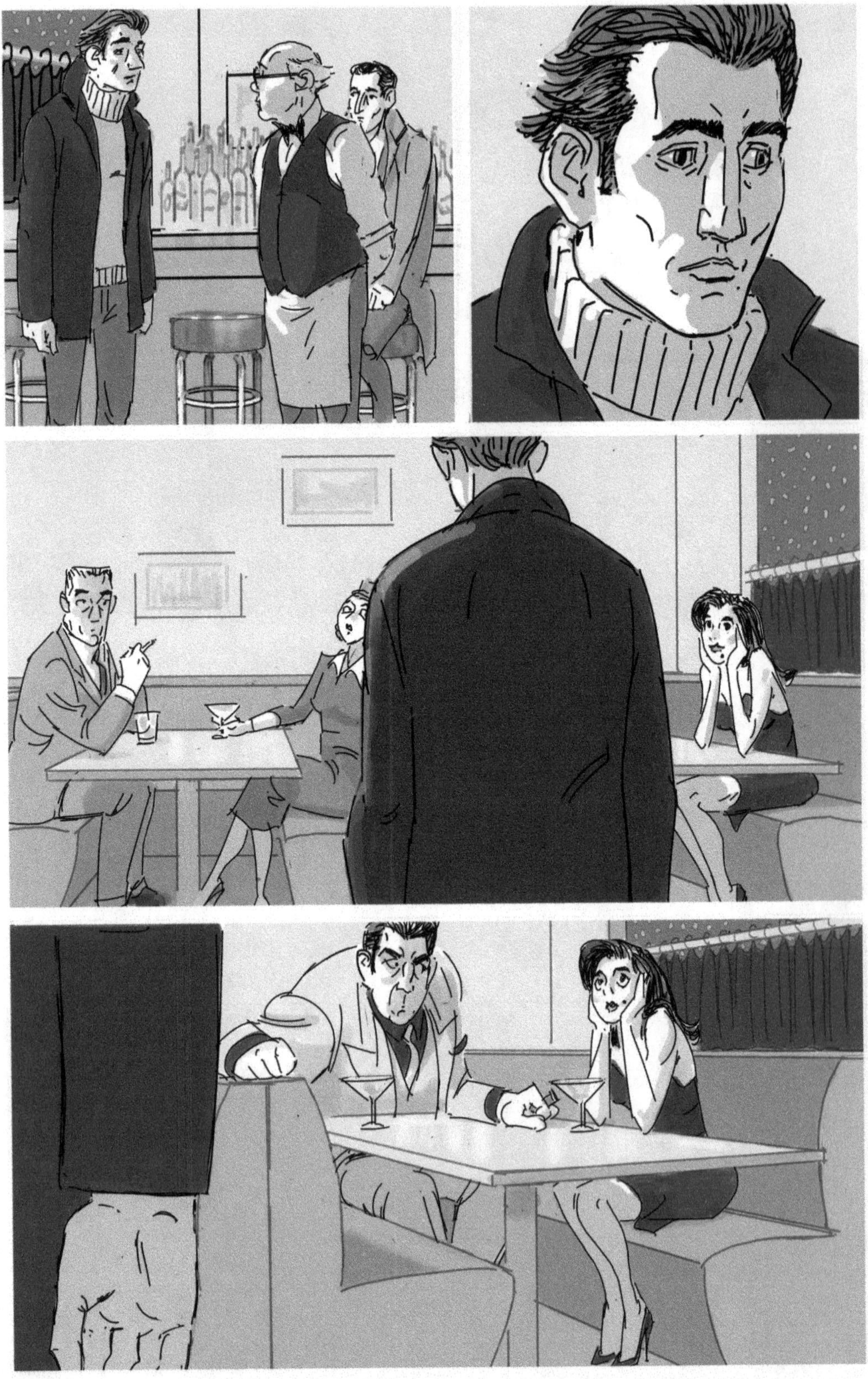

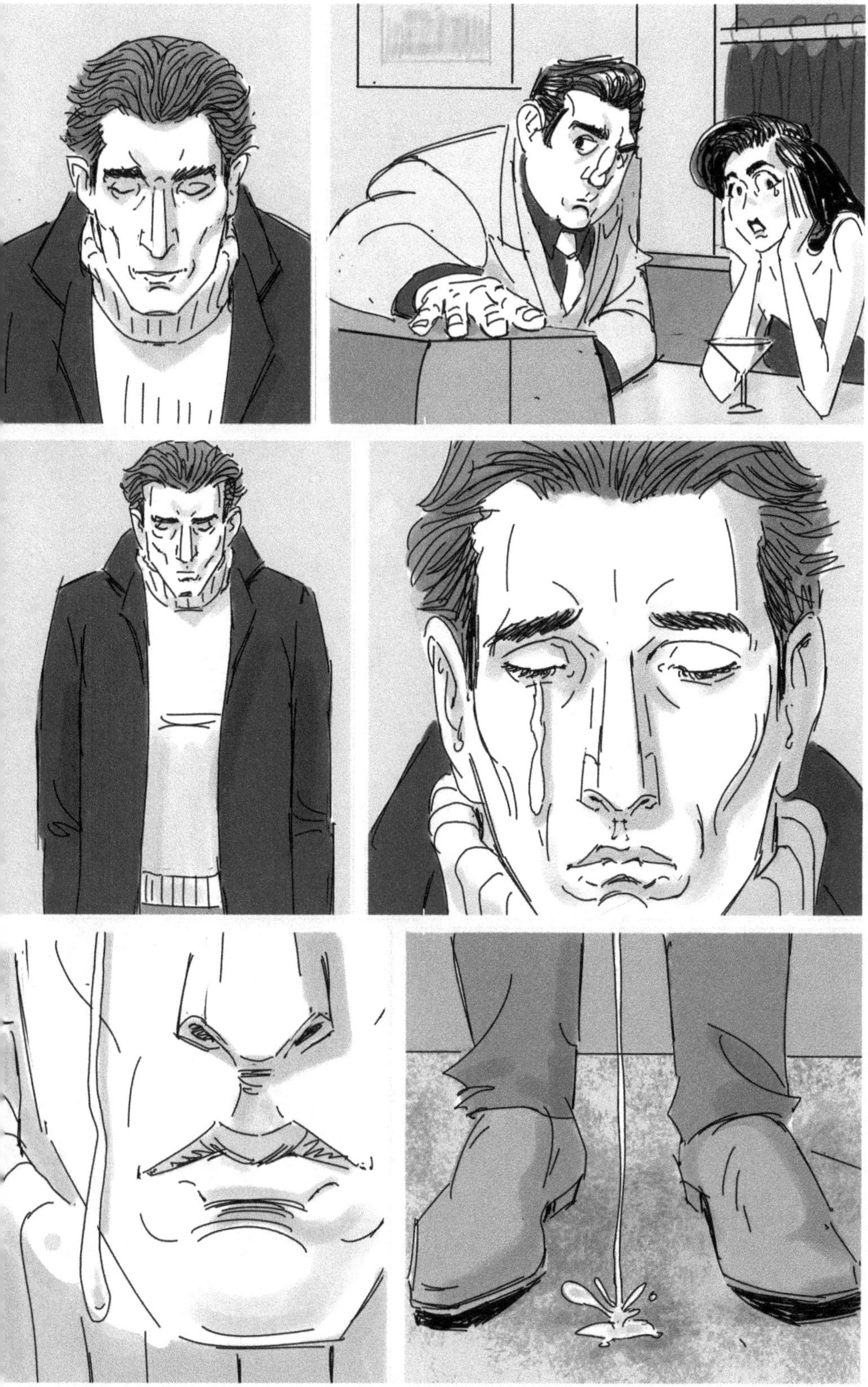

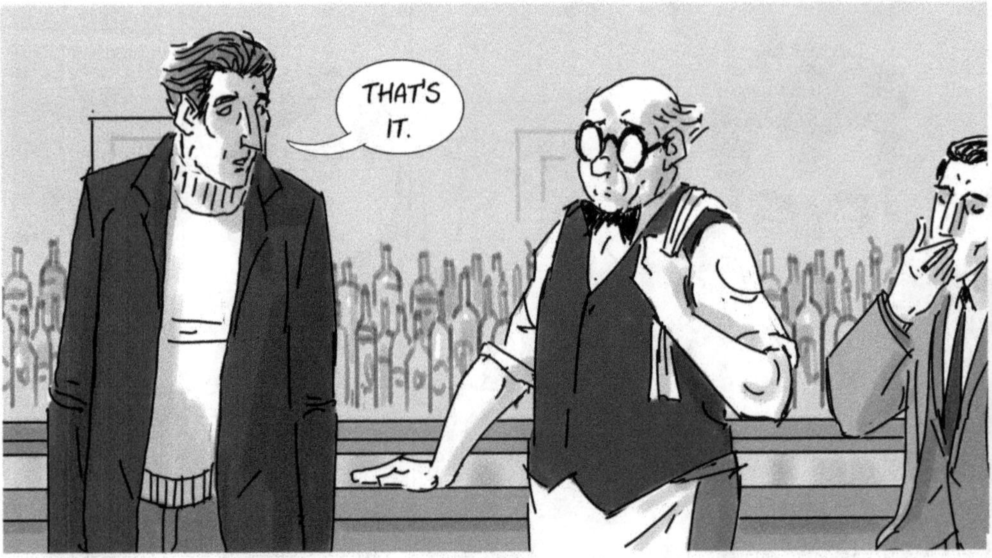
THAT'S IT.

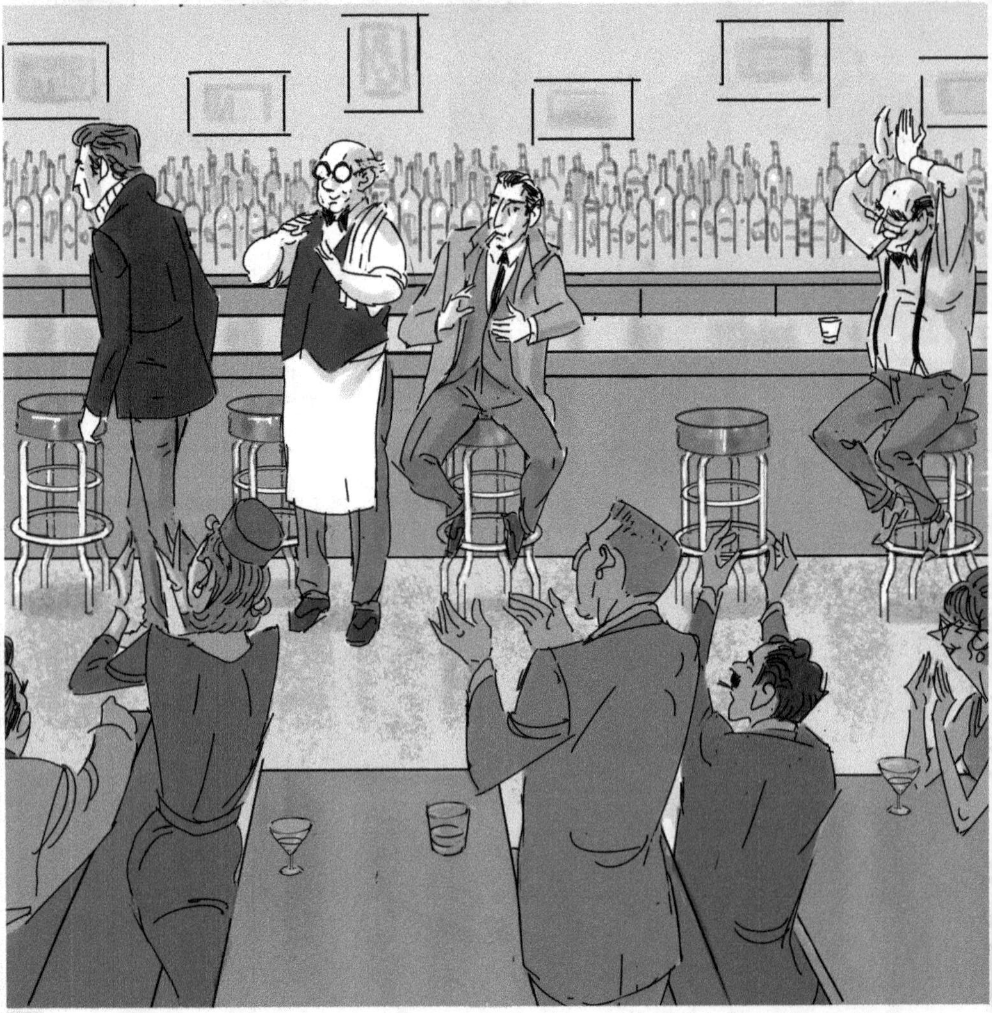

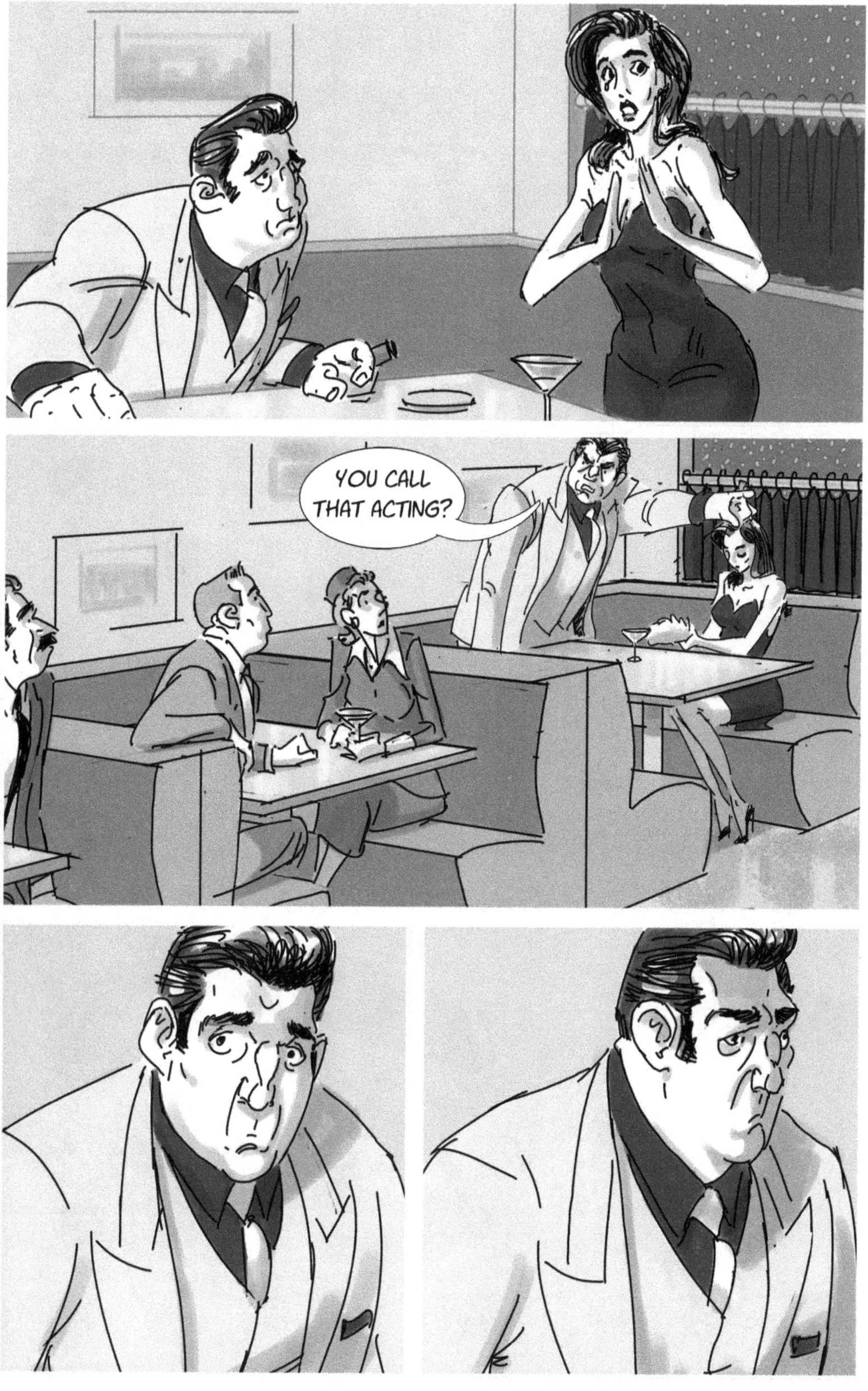
YOU CALL THAT ACTING?

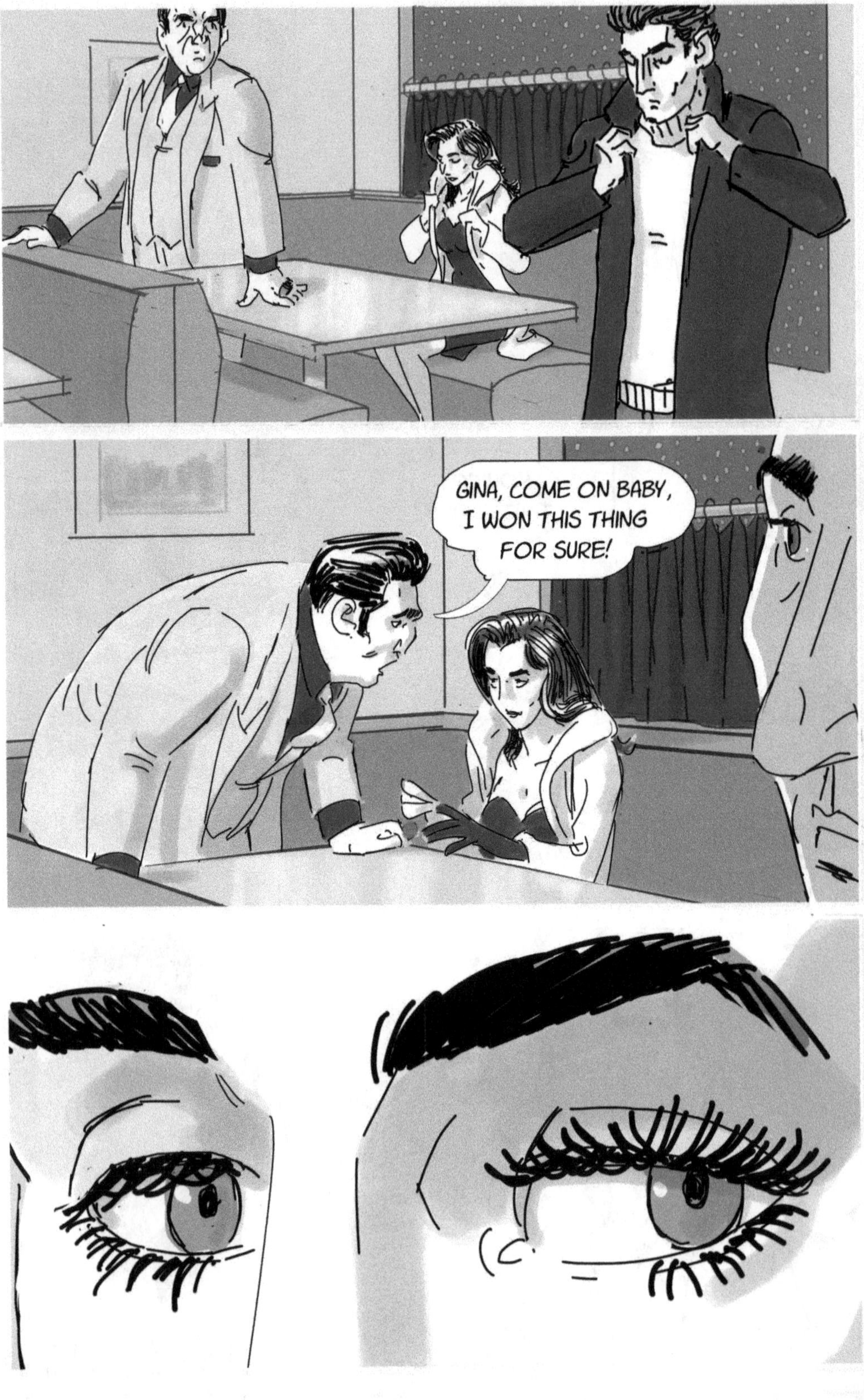
GINA, COME ON BABY, I WON THIS THING FOR SURE!

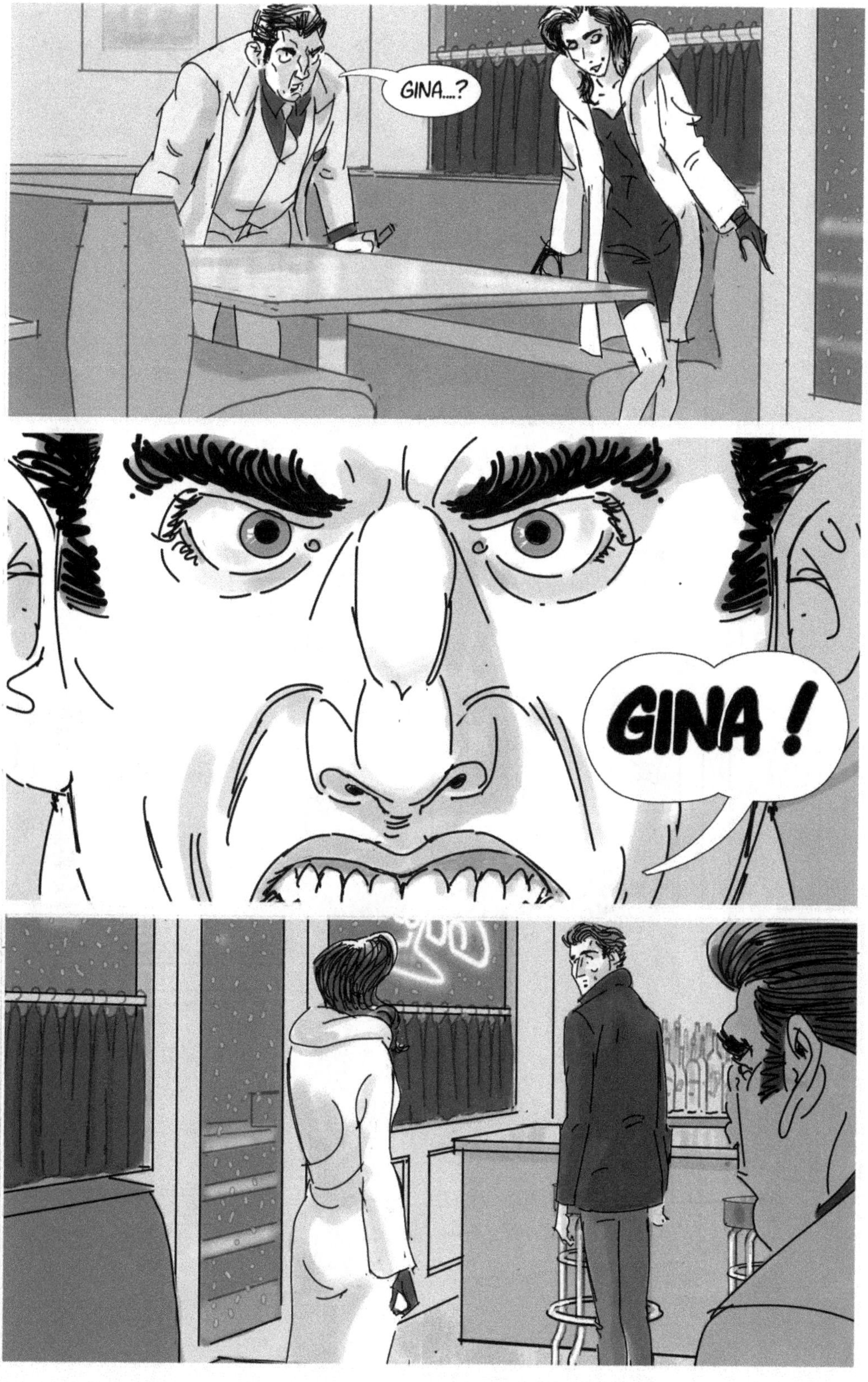
GINA...?
GINA !

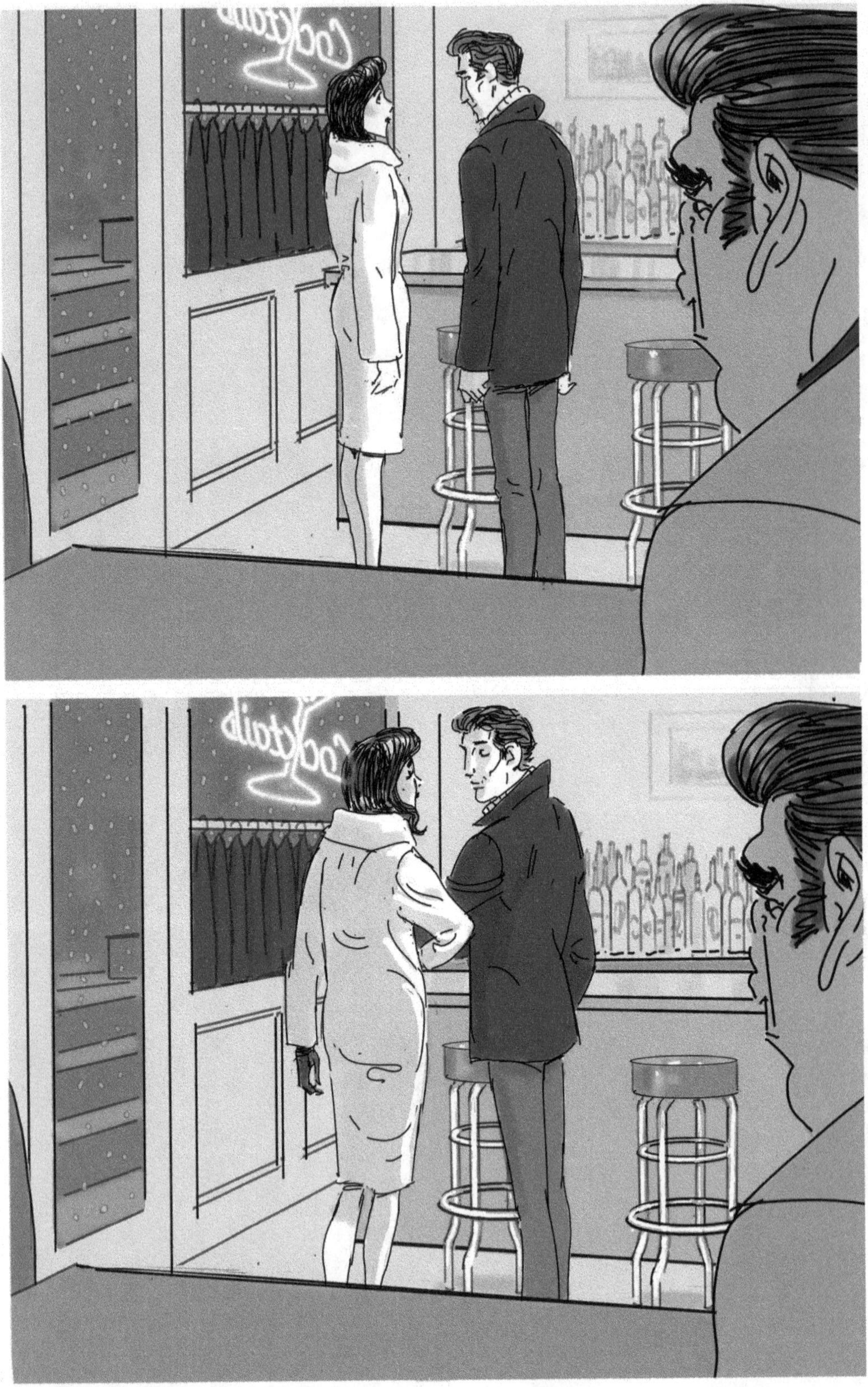
Cocktails
Cocktails

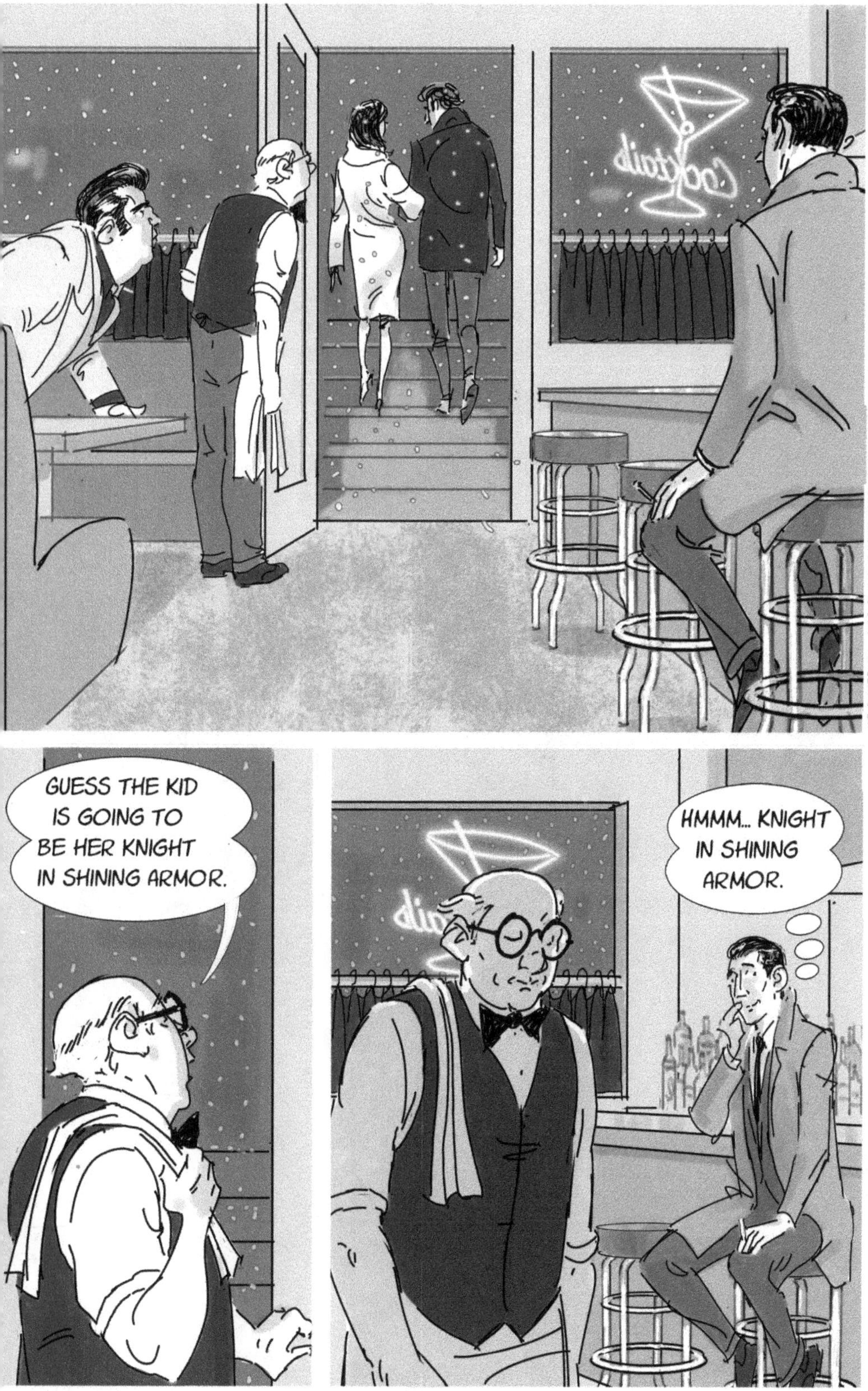
GUESS THE KID IS GOING TO BE HER KNIGHT IN SHINING ARMOR.
HMMM... KNIGHT IN SHINING ARMOR.

HAROLD'S SHOWSPOT
KNIGHT IN SHINING ARMOUR
DAMSEL IN DISTRESS
RESCUE!
HAROLD'S SHOWSPOT

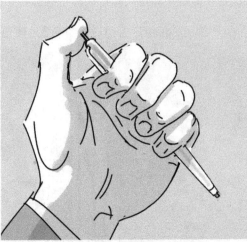

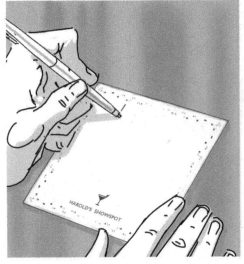

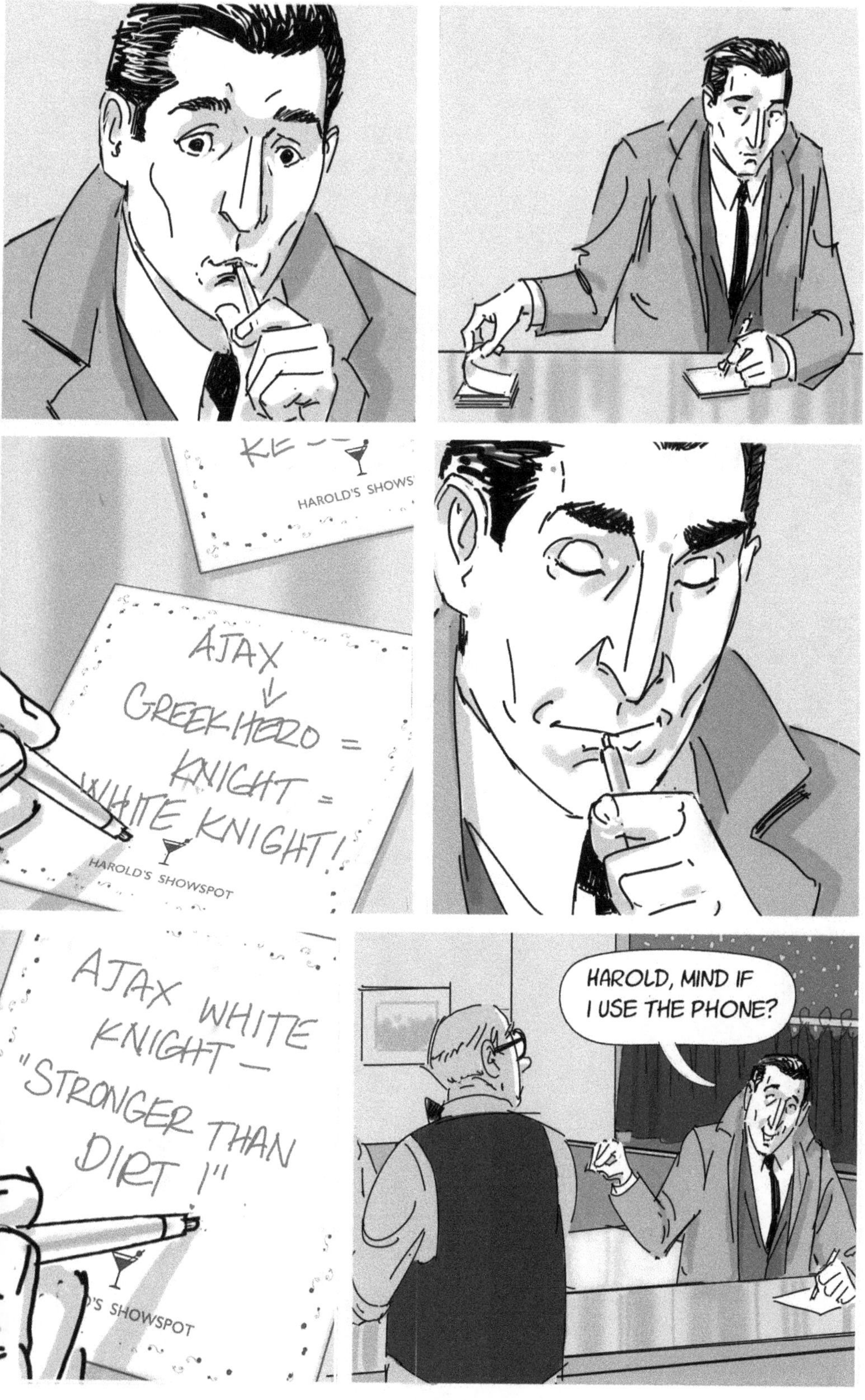
AJAX
GREEK HERO =
KNIGHT =
KNIGHT!
HAROLD'S SHOWSPOT
AJAX WHITE KNIGHT —
"STRONGER THAN DIRT!"
HAROLD, MIND IF I USE THE PHONE?

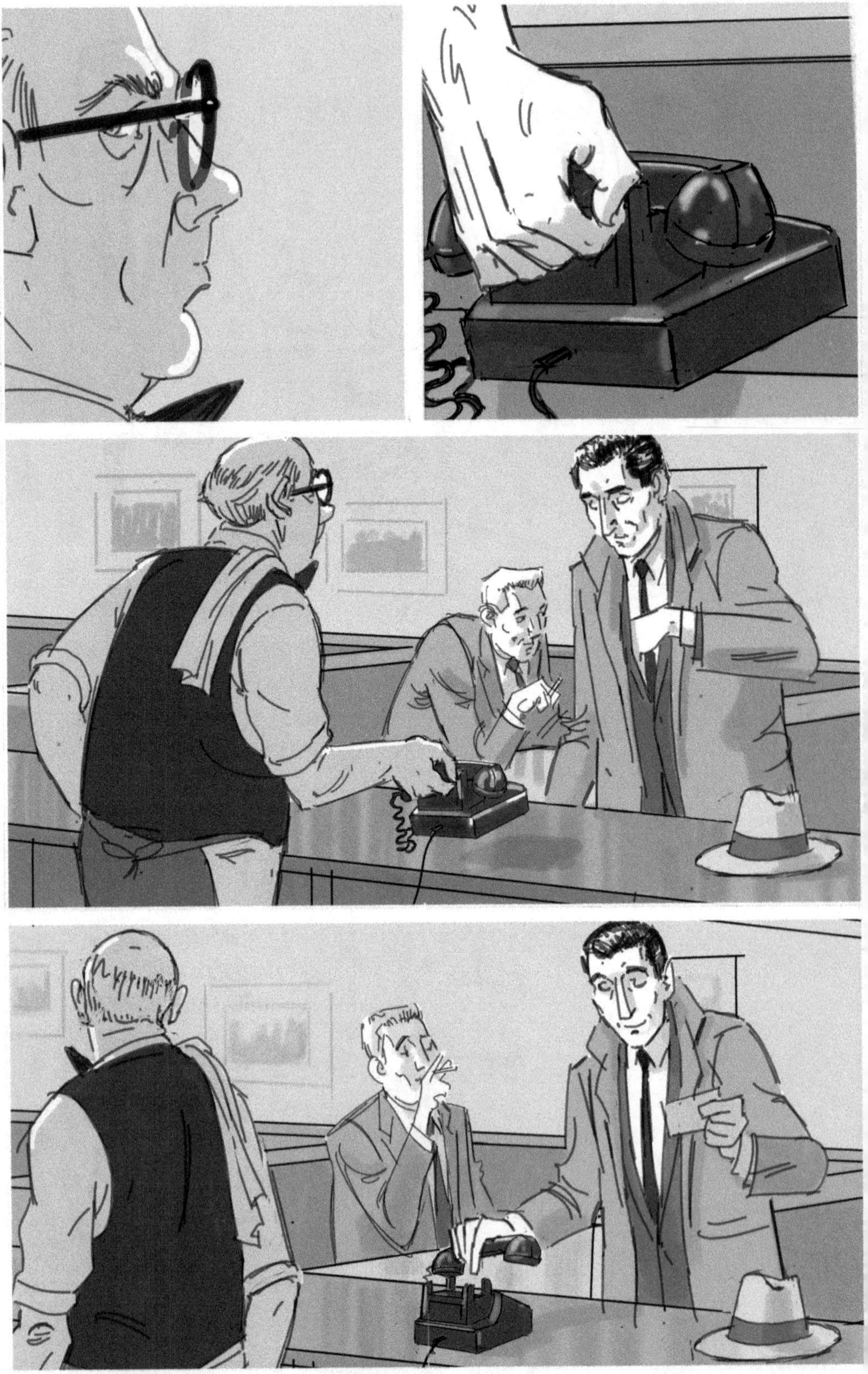

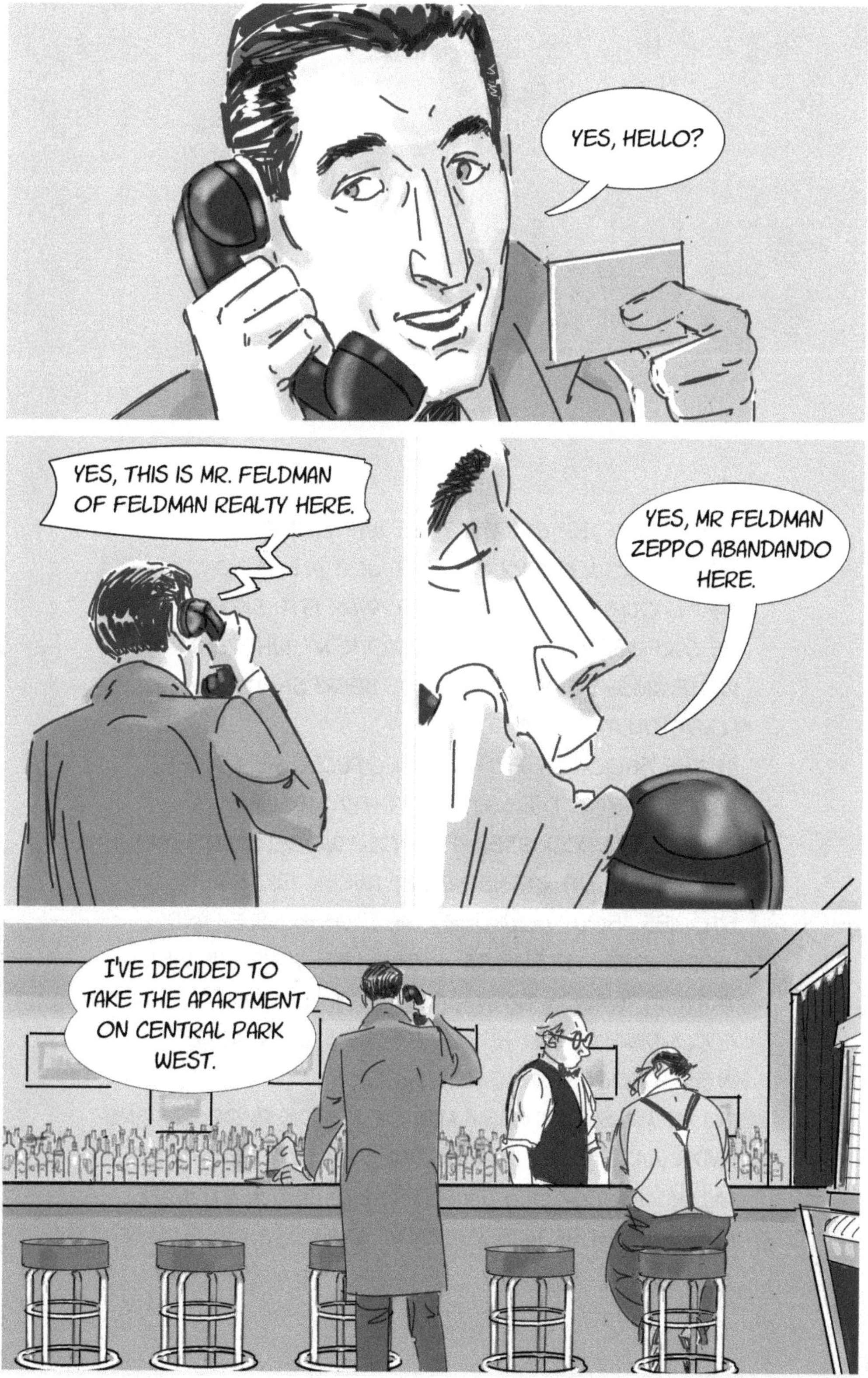
YES, HELLO?
YES, THIS IS MR. FELDMAN OF FELDMAN REALTY HERE.
YES, MR FELDMAN ZEPPO ABANDANDO HERE.
I'VE DECIDED TO TAKE THE APARTMENT ON CENTRAL PARK WEST.

SHORTLY AFTER CREATING THE WHITE KNIGHT CAMPAIGN
MY FATHER, JOE SACCO, GOT A JOB IN LONDON,
TAKING OUR FAMILY WITH HIM. FOR MY 13TH BIRTHDAY
HE SURPRISED ME WITH A TRIP TO KENT, WHERE A
WHITE KNIGHT COMMERCIAL WAS BEING SHOT ON
LOCATION AT BODIAM CASTLE.
AT THE SHOOT MY FATHER INTRODUCED ME TO THE
ACTOR PLAYING THE WHITE KNIGHT-TOM SWEET, A
RODEO BRONCO RIDER AND HOLLYWOOD STUNTMAN.
MR. SWEET ENTERTAINED ME BETWEEN TAKES WITH
STORIES ABOUT DOUBLING FOR ELVIS PRESLEY AND
WORKING ON TELEVISION SHOWS LIKE "HAVE GUN WILL
TRAVEL", "WAGON TRAIN" , AND "CIMARRON STRIP".
ACCORDING TO HIM, HE HAD BROKEN ALL 13 BONES
IN EACH FOOT DURING HIS CAREER.
TO ME MR. SWEET WAS A MAN OF HEROIC PROPORTIONS-
AND I WAS SAD TO LEARN SOME YEARS LATER THAT HE
AND HIS 10 YEAR OLD DAUGHTER HAD DIED IN A PRIVATE
PLANE CRASH. HE WAS 35 AT THE TIME.

MY FATHER DIED IN 1988, AGE 67. HIS NEW YORK TIMES
OBITUARY MADE MENTION OF THE MANY ICONIC AD CAMPAIGNS
HE CREATED THROUGHOUT HIS DECADES-LONG CAREER IN
ADVERTISING-SINGLING OUT THE ONE WITH THE "KNIGHT ON A
CHARGER WHOSE SWORD FLASHED WHITE TO SYMBOLIZE
HOUSEHOLD PURITY".
ONE CAN STILL VIEW A FEW OF THE OLD AJAX WHITE KNIGHT
COMMERCIALS, WHICH AIRED ON NETWORK TELEVISION
IN THE 1960'S, ON YOUTUBE.

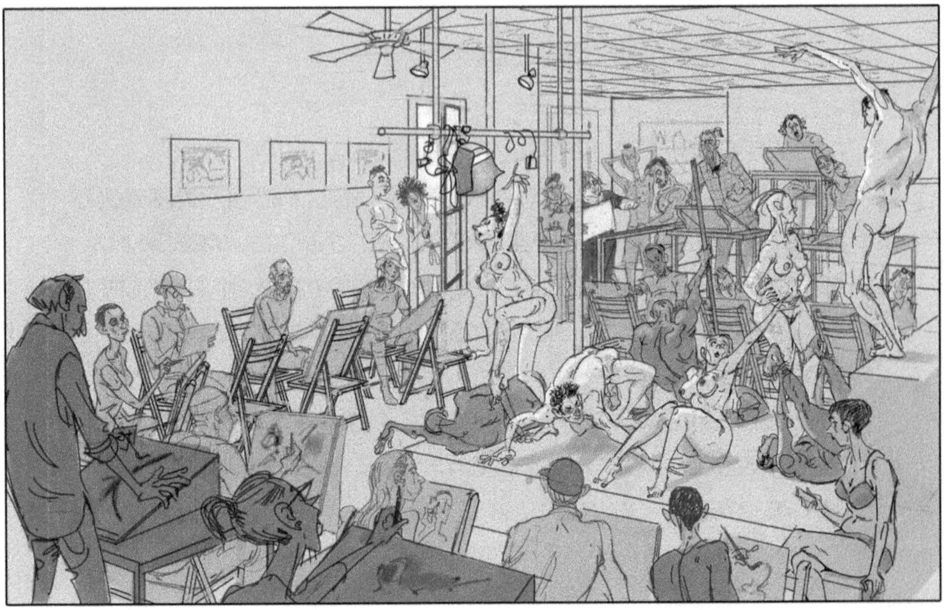


## ACKNOWLEDGEMENTS.

THANK YOU  JULES FEIFFER FOR YOUR THOUGHTFUL INSIGHTS.

THANK YOU TOM SACCHI , A NEW PAL WHO INTRODUCED ME TO THE FRENCH AND BELGIAN COMIC ARTISTS.

THANK YOU MINERVA DURHAM FOR SPRING STUDIO ,A PLACE FOR ARTISTS TO STUDY FIGURE DRAWING.

CPSIA information can be obtained
at www.ICGtesting.com
Printed in the USA
FSHW020009031019

9 781593 622930